Start & Run an
Event Planning Business

Start & Run an Event Planning Business

Cindy Lemaire and Mardi Foster-Walker

Self-Counsel Press
(*a division of*)
International Self-Counsel Press Ltd.
USA Canada

Printed in Canada.

Self-Counsel Press acknowledges the financial support of the Government of Canada through the Book Publishing Industry Development Program (BPIDP) for our publishing activities.

First edition: 2005

Library and Archives Canada Cataloguing in Publication

Foster-Walker, Mardi, 1952–
    Start & run an event-planning business / Mardi Foster-Walker, Cindy Lemaire.

    (Self-counsel business series)
    ISBN 1-55180-367-4

    1. Special events industry—Management. 2. New business enterprises. I. Lemaire, Cindy II. Title. III. Title: Start and run an event-planning business. IV. Series.

    GT3405.F68 2004   394.2'068   C2004-904489-3

A special thanks to Regan Hansen and Alan Walker for all their support and contributions during the writing of this book.

Self-Counsel Press
(a division of)
International Sclf-Counsel Press Ltd.

1704 N. State Street	1481 Charlotte Road
Bellingham, WA 98225	North Vancouver, BC V7J 1H1
USA	Canada

Contents

Introduction

Welcome to the world of owning your own special events business. You have taken an important first step by purchasing this book on how to own and operate your own special events company. The events business is big — really big. It is a $102.3 billion global industry according to Meeting Professionals International (MPI). Every day you will come across someone who is responsible for organizing an event, whether a special occasion such as a wedding, birthday party, graduation, or anniversary, or a major event such as a rock concert, film festival, fund-raising gala, convention, or awards ceremony. The world of event planning is an exciting one because the list of events being produced and celebrated every day is quite literally endless.

This industry is also a growing field. Projections show that, as an occupation, event planning and event management will outpace many others in the coming years. According to a joint study conducted by American Express and MPI, North America can expect to see employment growth of 3 percent and an increase of 5 percent in training budget in 2004, compared to 2003. The growth rate is attributed to an increase in related sectors, including international travel and tourism, business, and hospitality. Also, according to a Microsoft™ business website at <www.bcentral.com>, event planning businesses are among the top ten for ease of entry (start-up), low cost, future demand, and potentially high return. The need for qualified event planners grows in relation to the success of other sectors such as travel and tourism. When you launch your own company, the amount of business you generate for yourself is really all up to you.

A snapshot of the types of events that exist today will not do the industry justice, but it will help you to start narrowing down your focus. In this high-energy field, concentrating on one area of the business will help you focus your own resources. Start to think about the style of events that appeal to you. There are the formal occasions such as galas, awards banquets, and auctions. Then there are the business-focused events such as conferences, conventions, reward and recognition events (also known as incentives), and corporate meetings, and the industry-specific events such as expositions and trade shows. Plus, of course, there are the social events, which include a vast range of functions such as holiday celebrations, fund-raisers, weddings, sporting events, concerts, festivals, parades, children's activities, golf tournaments, and so on.

Even among the different types of events being produced, numerous specialties exist. Many in the business have found that their expertise is best concentrated on one specific aspect of producing an event. By focusing their business on what they do best, they improve their profitability. One could argue that there are as many kinds of work within the types of events as there are events themselves. From planning, coordinating, and managing to registration and on-site management, to production and volunteer organization, the many facets involved in this business will open up to you as you begin to get yourself established.

You are choosing a dynamic industry in which to make a living. Starting an event planning business is also fairly straightforward. There are no great barriers to entry, you do not need a lot of capital to get started, there are no secret formulas that need to be acquired, and the technology is readily available. This book will assist you to focus on your area of expertise; it will help you avoid becoming a jack-of-all-trades and specialist of none. Don't let yourself be overwhelmed. This guide will help you build your business one solid step at a time, laying the foundation for you to become a successful special event entrepreneur.

Maybe you have been planning events for years already. Perhaps you worked for an events company, a non-profit association or a large corporation. Maybe you've been volunteering your time planning and executing social events. Whether you already have events experience or are just starting out, this book will provide you with some basic skills for starting up an events business. You may have to take on smaller projects until you have developed the skills and experience to create the bigger events.

Regardless of your background, you have concluded that you have the skills, experience, and talent to venture out on your own. Or do you? Probably you have already discovered that you are detail oriented and self-motivated and will work beyond 9:00 a.m. to 5:00 p.m. You are most likely creative as well, which is important in this field. You want to run a business, therefore you have ambition, you are not afraid of rejection, and you are persistent. To run a business in this field you will also need to lead people, and that requires superb communication skills. Besides being creative, you must also be able to project a vision. If you don't possess these qualities yourself, you can carefully assemble a team that possesses them.

As you work through this book, you will be learning from professionals with more than 40 combined years of experience in running special events through their own businesses. You will learn marketing and operating skills to help you succeed more quickly than had you not done any research at all. It's a given that the people and businesses out there producing events do not have time to take risks. The organization or person contracting your company to coordinate an event will want to know why they should hire you over the competition. This book will provide you with the skills and know-how to stand out from your competitors and get the contracts.

As you plan your business, you will want to be connected to the internet and become familiar with webpage and brochure design. You will need to become familiar with database management and skilled at spreadsheet use. But keep in mind that this book is only a guideline. You will create brilliant strategies of your own. You will interact with other meeting planners — face-to-face, online, at trade shows, and through associations — and it will quickly become apparent that each may have a different approach. Remember that all of them started out just like you, with the basics. Now that you know how this book can help, let's get started!

1
Getting Started

Self-Assessment

What is it that makes one person succeed in the events industry while another fails? There is no one stereotype of a successful special events entrepreneur, but certain common characteristics can be found in those who succeed. For example, they are invariably hardworking, determined, resourceful, and capable of honest self-appraisal.

Starting your own special events business is risky, and you need to be clear on whether it is the best choice for you. You may already be working in the special events industry, but turning your skill into a business is a very different venture. Examining both your strengths and your weaknesses gives you the chance to remedy the factors that may impede your success. If you don't manage time well, don't like to work alone, and dislike making decisions, starting your own events business may not be appropriate — unless you are willing to work on your shortcomings. You don't have to be perfect, but you do need to recognize and acknowledge your strengths and weaknesses before investing time and money in a business.

To aid you in your self-analysis, a self-assessment test is provided here for your use (see Worksheet 1). It outlines some characteristics for success in this field and asks you to evaluate yourself against them. Answer the questions honestly to determine how many success characteristics you already have. This test will not definitively tell you what you should do, but it can help you engage in honest self-appraisal. A passion to succeed, an eagerness to learn, and an acceptance of responsibility can overcome any weaknesses.

The value of any quiz, test, or questionnaire lies in that it can help you identify your strengths and admit your weaknesses. Look on this self-appraisal as an important first step in your journey to starting and running a successful special events business. You are capable of capitalizing on your strengths and compensating for your weaknesses as long as you know what they are and if your desire to do so is powerful enough.

Once you have determined that starting a special events business is the right venture for you, take some time to test your ability to create special events. If you have not created events before, we recommend that you create on paper two or three theme events. Organize them in a portfolio with sketches, photos, fabric swatches, menus, rental details, production schedules, and budgets. Use this portfolio of event ideas when doing your market research by showing them to family and friends.

Determining Your Market

Once you have decided on whether or not this field is right for you, your next step is to determine your market or area of specialty. Is there a big enough market waiting to hire you to produce their special events? Make certain you discover this before you risk time and money on starting a business.

Many start-up operations are established solely on instinct and optimism. The enthusiastic new business owner may have only a vague idea about who his or her clients are or, indeed, whether or not there will be any clients at all. Operating on blind faith, such people are relying on plain old luck to see them through, and sometimes, it takes just that. However, while every business needs a little luck now and then, banking on it is hazardous to the long-term health of your enterprise.

The special events industry is so vast that the event organizer is not limited to just one market segment. Even those who are experts

WORKSHEET 1
SELF-ASSESSMENT TEST

Check the appropriate column for each of the following statements.
(N = never; M = most of the time; A = always)

	N	M	A
1. I am a self-starter.	___	___	___
2. I am normally positive and optimistic.	___	___	___
3. I easily accept personal responsibility.	___	___	___
4. I have no problem working alone.	___	___	___
5. I am competitive.	___	___	___
6. I commit strongly.	___	___	___
7. I am flexible.	___	___	___
8. I am self-confident.	___	___	___
9. I relate well to other people.	___	___	___
10. I am a goal setter.	___	___	___
11. I am a creative problem solver.	___	___	___
12. I like to plan.	___	___	___
13. I am a decision maker.	___	___	___
14. I enjoy working hard.	___	___	___
15. I can tolerate risk.	___	___	___
16. I seldom procrastinate.	___	___	___
17. I am innovative.	___	___	___
18. I handle stress well.	___	___	___
19. I am independent by nature.	___	___	___
20. I am a logical thinker.	___	___	___
21. I am persistent.	___	___	___
22. I communicate well with others.	___	___	___
23. I manage my time well.	___	___	___
24. I have plenty of common sense.	___	___	___
25. I have the ability to think objectively.	___	___	___
26. I am in good health.	___	___	___
27. I like to learn new things.	___	___	___
28. I am realistic.	___	___	___
29. I can take criticism.	___	___	___
30. I am ambitious.	___	___	___

Now determine your score. Should you start your own business? Count your **Always** and **Most of the time** answers as positive. If you scored

30 out of 30	You should be running General Motors.
26 – 29	You've got what it takes.
21 – 25	You'll do just fine.
16 – 20	Be sure you answered yes to number 14 and 27.
15	Questionable.
Under 15	Unlikely, but nothing is impossible.

in the events business will have a difficult time trying to define all the potential markets. But to be successful in a field that is so broad, you need to find your niche — a specialty that combines your best capabilities with a service that is necessary and, preferably, under-served in your area. As outlined in the introduction, the choices are plentiful: conferences, conventions, incentives, corporate meetings, expositions, trade shows, fund-raisers, weddings, sporting events, concerts, festivals, parades, children's events, golf tournaments, and the list goes on. When you concentrate on one market, referrals and word-of-mouth businesses come your way much more quickly. On the flip side, when you work in different fields and functions, you reduce your chances to become known as the best in the business.

Where do you see yourself? What makes sense to you and the community you plan to serve? You may need some experience to gain this insight, but what's important is to keep your options open and remember that you cannot succeed if you spread your special events business too thin. The key to your success is to identify your potential customers, to know what they want, and to determine how to fill that need.

Market Research

Your market is that segment of the population that could potential-ly use your service. Finding out who they are and what they want is called market research. This research will provide you with the data you need to help identify your potential clients and determine how to reach them. Conducting thorough market research is the foundation of any successful business.

First, you must research your competition. Any special events company that is doing serious business will be advertised in the Yellow Pages and will likely have a website. Spend time looking at your competitors' websites and studying their printed materials. This should give you a good idea of who the major players in the marketplace are and the type of competition you are up against. Remember that these people may be your competitors now, but there is a good possibility that they will become your future col-leagues — people who will refer clients to you and people with whom you may associate professionally to share information on growing your businesses. It is not in your best interest to pretend to be a customer and waste another event professional's time asking for quotes or ideas. This type of behavior can return to haunt you.

Competition is not a deterrent to going into business. However, it is important to know who your competitors are and where they are located so that you are on an equal footing. Knowing your competition allows you to learn from them. What do they do right? What do they do wrong? How will you be better?

Market research helps confirm market size, minimize financial risk, save time, and pinpoint where you should concentrate your service. Researching your market can also uncover market segments that you may not have originally considered. It establishes a foundation for decision-making and positioning your service. However, not taking the time to do some basic market research can cause you to fail when you might otherwise have succeeded.

The steps in basic market research are outlined here.

Set a realistic time limit

Decide how much time you intend to devote to market research and stick to that time limit. Think in terms of normal working days and eliminate weekends. Do not become so caught up in doing research that it takes precedence over getting the business started.

Define your information needs

What do you need to know? By properly defining your needs, you can save valuable time and avoid having to cope with too much information. To give your special events business a realistic chance of success, and to have the information necessary to write a comprehensive business plan, you must define what data is relevant for your proposed business.

When you are starting out, you should collect information about the following aspects of the industry:

(a) Number of potential markets

(b) Size of each market

(c) Market trends

(d) Demographics of the clients served within markets

(e) Competitive companies

(f) Market share

Within the market as a whole, you will also want to identify demographics, industry outlook, growth potential, economic trends, population shifts, consumer trends, and relevant economic indicators.

For example, if your proposed business is located in an area with a convention center, you could consider convention management, trade shows, event or conference registration, and spousal programs as potential markets and gather all relevant data. The size of the market is the number of meetings and conventions booked each year. Market trends would be the size of the conventions, conferences, and trade shows booked and the types of associations, industries, and corporations booking the facility. Your target customers would be the decision-makers at the companies who organize the meetings and events. Competitive companies are the number of other companies in your area that offer their special events services to the convention center. Market share is the percentage of the convention center special events you realistically think you could attain.

Allocate resources

Your resources for market research are personnel and funds. If you are starting a business with a partner or if a family member is available, delegate tasks and responsibilities and try not to step on each other's toes. One person could make phone calls while the other goes to the library. If you are not already set up at home with a computer and an internet connection, this is the time to install this equipment. See chapter 3 for more information on getting set up.

Much of the information-gathering will require time, but the cash required should be minimal. However, be prepared to spend some money, for government reports and publications on industry trends and statistics may be of interest, and many of them cost money.

Gather the data

Identify and contact the most appropriate sources for the information you need. Organize and file your research results as they accumulate. Don't keep unnecessary data, and do keep an eye on your projected completion date. The following are some good sources of information, from the general to the more targeted:

The internet

The internet provides a wealth of information at your fingertips. Start by using a good search engine. (Yahoo!, Google, and AOL are among the top picks.) Your local bookstore or library should be able to supply you with some great search tips, if you are not that familiar with search tools. Once you become acquainted with internet research, you will find this method will save you time on the phone and in your car, as much of the research legwork can be done on your computer. Be careful to check your sources — links from recognized organizations (chambers of commerce, government, Better Business Bureau, etc.) are your best bets for starting out, as not everything on the internet is credible information. Your local government or chamber of commerce will also provide you with community and business links to lead you to the information you need.

Your local library

Libraries are invaluable resources. Look through business and trade publications for trends and sales information. Often you can find market studies on file that directly fit your needs. You can also locate census information and trade reports. Ask the librarian for help with your specific information needs.

The Yellow Pages

Your local telephone book can be a major resource. Study the classifications that list your competitors under the headings Special Event Planners, Wedding Planners, Party Planners, and so on. How many competitors are there and do they use display advertising?

Chamber of commerce

Your local chamber of commerce is an excellent source for all business information. Visit them online, call them, or visit them in person. If they cannot help you, they will direct you to someone who can.

College or university business departments

Many college and university business departments offer extensive research help to the new businessperson. Occasionally, advanced students will take on the complete market research function for a company as a research project.

Government departments

Government departments, particularly those devoted to small-business development, can be another helpful source of information. In the United States, the Small Business Administration (SBA) offers publications covering topics such as budgeting, market research, legal structures, marketing, and financing. Call your local office and ask a counselor what is available. In Canada, these departments are the responsibility of each province. The department that handles small-business development can provide information on start-up assistance and point you to federal programs that may be helpful.

Both federal and provincial or state governments are increasingly using "portal" technology to better guide their online users. Through these portal websites, governments direct you by your area of interest to the relevant resources and portfolios available, both online and in print. These sites offer reliable links to business sites within government. Go to <www.state.gov> or <www.whitehouse.gov> for the US government portals. The Government of Canada's portal is at <www.gc.ca>.

The Business Development Bank of Canada (BDC) <www.bdc.ca> conducts seminars on business topics, which are very informative to anyone new to business. It also offers books and pamphlets. (Go to <http://www.sba.gov/bi/bics/referencematerial.html> on the internet for a complete listing of the topics covered.) There is a charge for most of these publications. If you do not have a BDC office near you, write to the nearest regional office.

If you need demographics, the BDC's online computer service has it all. Again, if you do not use a computer with an internet connection, you should get set up now. Otherwise, you can engage the services of a research firm to help you with your search, but keep in mind that these services can be expensive.

The face-to-face meeting

Perhaps the most effective way to gather data is to arrange personal meetings with people who are potential sources of information. A representative from your local chamber of commerce, the head of a trade association, an executive from a hotel, the owner of a travel agency, and a corporate executive are a few examples of people who could provide you with valuable information. More than any other information-gathering activity, face-to-face meetings often lead to other important sources for data and will often establish business contacts that could be important to you in the future.

Remember that in the events world, you may have to meet with several departments in larger organizations. For example, individual departments may be responsible for their own events (sales and marketing division versus research and design), and they may even have responsibility for different aspects of one event (planning versus operations). Again, the internet is a great place to start doing some background research on the companies you have targeted. Look for up-to-date information on events or meetings or media. Often, there is a contact name listed. Review the news releases and calendars if they are available. Do an online search to find out if the company has networking associations with other companies.

Telephone well in advance to schedule a face-to-face meeting. Know the name and proper title of the person you want to see and use it during your conversation. Introduce yourself and briefly indicate what you would like to talk about. People are busy, so don't waste time or talk about your plans in too much detail.

Try to gather as much information as possible before you meet face-to-face. Once you have conducted this initial research, you will be better equipped to pose questions that are relevant to the person you are interviewing. Refer to the information you have collected and ask for specifics. Here are some basic questions to ask during a personal interview with a potential client for your business:

(a) Does their company currently hire special events professionals?

(b) How often do they hire special events professionals?

(c) What type of events do they put on?

(d) Are they satisfied with the quality and cost of the events?

(e) What are their event objectives that must be met?

(f) Do they see their event needs changing in the near future (for example, special occasions coming up, such as a company anniversary, new associations or expansions, change of venue)?

(g) Do they have associations with other organizations that do events or partner on events?

(h) What sources do they use to find event professionals?

The more questions you ask, the better understanding you will have of your potential clients and exactly what they are looking for. Bring a portfolio with several of the special event ideas that you have produced or created. Write down information as the meeting progresses. Refer to your notes and ask questions to be certain that you get the information you need. Ask for a referral to another source for information. If possible, hand the person a card with your name and number and ask for a call of introduction.

After the meeting, review what you have learned, rewrite your notes, and file them. Always follow up by contacting referrals, and always remember to send a thank-you note after a face-to-face meeting. One of the most important things to keep in mind when planning for and operating your business is the follow-up. Those you meet with today to collect market research may be the companies and individuals you do business with later on. Always take the opportunity to make a lasting impression on your future clients by sending them a formal thank-you note for their time and assistance, including your name and contact information.

Analyze the information

Study the information you have collected as objectively as possible. Ask yourself the following questions:

(a) Is there a market for your service?

(b) Can you define who your potential clients are?

(c) Do you know who your competitors are?

(d) Can you see any advantage your service will have over your competitors?

(e) Do you know your competitors' prices?

(f) Do you know where your clients are?

(g) Are there enough clients to sustain your business?

(h) Do you know how to sell and market your service?

(i) Can you afford to be on the same playing field with your competition (i.e., are you in the same league)?

(j) Can you price your services competitively and still make a profit?

Weigh your findings against your original idea. Does the data suggest a slight deviation from that plan? Does it affirm or negate your business premise? Cull from the data what fits best with your experience, resources, creativity, and preference. Based on this information, you can define your service. Then date the material and file it for future reference. Save any remaining research information that backs up your business idea.

Once you feel you can comfortably answer yes to these ten questions, the next step is to research a location for your new business and an operation site within that location.

2
Establishing Your Business Site

Location Considerations

Once you have determined your market and are confident about your special event business, you need to find space from which you can operate. The two options covered in this section are finding and working from an office space and setting up a home-based operation.

Leasing Office or Studio Space

If your dwelling is not appropriate for a home-based business and you have enough capital to rent an outside space, you can consider leasing office or studio space. The advantage to leasing outside space is that you can invite potential clients to meet with you there.

Additionally, clients often presume that those operating outside of the home are the more successful, established organizations. This presumption, of course, is not appreciated by the many within the events field who do work out of their homes. Certainly choosing this option has the advantage of the professional image it lends to your company. Many large corporate accounts will feel more comfortable doing business with a company in an office building.

When leasing office or studio space, it is a good idea to consider the following issues:

(a) Proximity and accessibility to potential clients

(b) Parking facilities

(c) Accessibility to loading dock or freight elevator

(d) Work space and storage

(e) Type of lease agreement

(f) Shared space

(g) Security system

(h) Proximity to coffee shops, food places, or convenience stores

Proximity and accessibility to potential clients

Consider how close any potential office space is to your clientele. Make it easy for your clients to find you.

Parking facilities

Make sure you locate your office where there is plenty of free or inexpensive parking for the convenience of your clients, delivery trucks, and staff.

Accessibility to a loading dock or freight elevator

If you start to store collateral and props prior to an event, you will be grateful for easy access to a loading bay or freight elevator.

Work space and storage

Make sure your office has sufficient space for storing supplies and meeting with clients. You can lease your own space in an office building, small-business park, warehouse, or loft/studio space. Storage space will depend on the type of events you will work on and whether or not you will choose to purchase and store props.

Another option is the "packaged office." This type of facility usually takes up the entire floor of an office building. Each company has one office space. There is one central reception area and a receptionist who can accept deliveries, take messages, and perform secretarial services for a separate fee. These offices generally have a photocopy machine and fax machine available, which all the tenants share. However, there may be cost and privacy issues when operating in such a facility. You need to ensure that your clients and suppliers will be treated well by the other businesses sharing the same office space.

Type of lease agreement

If you rent or lease space, you will need to decide what kind of lease agreement you are willing to sign. The longer the lease term, the lower the monthly rent, but you are responsible for the full term of the lease whether you are still operating the business or not. Some lease agreements will not allow you to sublet the space.

For a brand-new business, it is probably best to take a one-year lease or month-to-month rent at a higher rate until you have ascertained how well your business is going to do. Always seek competent legal advice before signing any kind of lease agreement to be sure you understand the fine print.

Before renting or leasing space, ask yourself the following questions:

(a) Is the space accessible for receiving and shipping?

(b) Is there a loading bay? What about elevators?

(c) Is there sufficient parking for delivery trucks and clients?

(d) Are there enough electrical power outlets for your equipment?

(e) Is the lighting, heating, and air conditioning sufficient?

(f) Will your lease allow you to make necessary alterations, such as installing work spaces?

(g) What type of advertising sign is permissible in your lease agreement?

(h) How safe is the area and the building?

(i) Will you be able to buy reasonable insurance against burglary and fire?

Home-Based Operation

Being able to work from home is often a deciding factor for those starting a business. For many would-be entrepreneurs, working from home is the most economical way to get started. In the event business, there are plenty of home-based operations.

You can't choose your space in the same way you would if you were looking for space to rent or lease. However, if you do decide to run the business from your home, you will need to make sure you do not violate zoning ordinances or rental agreements (if you do not own your home). If you have space to run a home-based business, you should still spend some time researching the cost of office/studio space. This will give you an indication of what rental costs would be incurred if you ran your business in another location. Paying yourself the equivalent rent each month will give you a better indication of your profitability and the feasibility of future expansion.

Every home-based business is a unique blend of family, skills, and lifestyle. To make the blend rich and prosperous, each must be considered independently. Will your business suit your home environment? Do you have sufficient space to work undisturbed? Does working from home suit your personal style? Can you stand to be away from the buzz of a workplace? Can you be motivated while home-based distractions such as laundry, dishes, social visits, television, and sleep surround you? Think about these questions carefully.

The business and your home

Ideally, you should have a separate room for your business so that, at the end of the workday, you can shut the door (and lock it from inquisitive children). There needs to be enough space for your working needs as well as any supplies and materials you will store. Walk through your home with new eyes and visualize where you could set up a place of business. Many residential floor plans make no allowances for work space.

See if there is enough privacy. You need to work uninterrupted. Figure out where your business telephone will be. You must be able to have uninterrupted telephone conversations — they are essential to your business. A door ensures that you can separate your business from housework.

Think about noise. Will your business create intolerable noise or will other people's noise be intolerable for your business? Most inside doors are hollow and easily allow sound to pass through. If there is potential friction over noise, it may be worthwhile to install a solid core door.

Your business should be compatible with the area you live in and cause no annoyance to your neighbors. Some area residents have closed down home-based businesses they viewed as a nuisance. In the events business, you will be meeting with suppliers and clients often, and taking up all the allotted street or visitor parking can annoy neighbors.

Remember to consider your family situation. How will you deal with child care, chores, and time with your spouse, friends, and others?

Whether or not you decide to base your business in your home also depends on the zoning restrictions in your community and the rental agreement you have with your landlord if you do not own your residence. See chapter 10 for more on zoning laws and rental agreements.

Consider your company image. There has been much growth in the number of home-based businesses in recent years, and the idea has become much more widely accepted. However, some people will not take seriously a business operating out of the home, and it is important to follow a few guidelines that will make your home-based business look more professional.

For instance, install a separate telephone line and do not let children or other family members answer that line. If you are unable to take a call, use an answering machine or a voice messaging service. Use a post office box number as your business address if your home address is obviously a residential area or an apartment building.

If you anticipate having clients visit your home office, make sure you have a designated space, close to the entrance, that is only for business and decorated accordingly. If you do not have that type of space available, it might be wise to avoid meeting clients at your home. Meet them outside your home office, such as at their place of business or coffee shops.

The primary advantage to running a business out of your home is the small capital outlay necessary to get started. Having lower overhead will allow you to invest more money in promoting and marketing your business.

A home-based business also carries numerous tax advantages. To take full advantage of these tax breaks, your home-based operation must take up an entire room that is devoted solely to your business. These tax advantages are discussed in further detail in chapter 11.

The business and your family

Most often, the spouse who chooses to work at home is the one with primary responsibility for child care. Blending the two tasks is no easy matter, particularly with very young children. The needs of the children and the demands of the business are often at odds with each other.

Consider the following options to address challenges:

(a) Work around your children's schedules

(b) Work while your children are in school

(c) Hire in-home care

(d) Take your children to out-of-home care

Your need for child care while running your business will depend on several factors, notably your financial objectives, the time required to meet those objectives, and the ages of your children. The children, however, regardless of age, will be affected by your decision to start your business from the home. Tell your children as openly as you can about your plans. Younger children need to understand, for example, that your supplies are not available for their artwork. Older children can understand the importance of your work and help out by assuming more household duties.

Although it is crucial to explain to family members the importance of your work, it is equally crucial that you balance the time between your work and family. It is sometimes difficult to leave a home-based business behind. Many home-based business operators find themselves going back to work after dinner, late at night, or on weekends.

For your sake and that of your family, don't turn yourself into a home workaholic. Turn off the ringer on your phone after hours, and really consider a separate, self-contained work space. Closing that door at the end of your work time gives you a clear dividing line between work and family needs.

3
Business Resources and Equipment

As mentioned earlier, you need very little equipment to start up a special events business, but you do need some basic office equipment and services in place. This chapter discusses how to establish the basics for your business and provides options to consider so you can control your expenses. With a thorough review and comparison of the costs of the main overhead areas, you should require only a small capital investment and keep your overhead and risk to a minimum.

Business Resources

This section reviews the basic resources you'll need to run your business, and addresses some issues you'll need to consider before making your decisions on which resources you'll require.

Mailbox and copy services

If your office space is in your home, or if the space you lease or rent doesn't have an office image, rent a post office box from a private mailbox rental outlet that offers a street address and suite number.

This will allow you to have a suite number on your address and will present a more professional image. Most communities and neighborhoods have private postal outlets, and you will find them convenient for a number of reasons. These outlets offer some or all of the following services:

- 24-hour mailbox service with street address and suite number
- Mail receiving/forwarding
- Stamps and metered mail
- Packing, shipping, and supplies
- All forms of shipping — overnight, second day air, ground
- Fax service
- Secretarial services
- Photocopies
- Money transfers
- Money orders
- Telephone messaging/voice mail
- Business cards and stationery
- Office/shipping supplies

Having this type of business close by can be very advantageous, especially in the start-up phase of your company. Look in the Yellow Pages under Mail Boxes, Postal Box Rentals, or Postal Services to find an appropriate facility in your area.

Business telephone line and fax line

A business telephone line is more expensive than a regular personal line, but it is necessary if you want to be listed in the Yellow Pages and in the white pages under your company name. When you subscribe, be prepared to show your business license and/or incorporation documents. Depending on your credit rating, you may also be required to pay a refundable deposit.

For a start-up special events business, a single telephone line and a designated fax line should be sufficient. It is a good idea to invest in a separate line and number for your fax machine. You don't want your telephone line tied up by the fax machine. Also, there are many business fax machines that cannot connect to fax lines that are hooked up with a phone line or answering machine. We also recommend a separate line for a high-speed internet connection, since so much of business today is conducted online and by e-mail. As your business grows, you may want to invest in a multi-line phone system, which allows you to have two or more calls coming in or going out simultaneously. The hookup fees and monthly charges for this type of service are expensive; you should wait to see if the volume of business calls you receive warrants the costs. However, if you are purchasing new phones for your business, it might be wise to purchase multi-line phones ahead of the service, as the cost of these phones isn't much greater than that for single-line phones.

Telephone and wireless communication options

The options for staying connected with your clients are growing by the day, but for now you will still want to invest in the basics: a telephone system. When you choose your telephone system, remember it is an essential piece of business equipment. You need to think about the impression your telephone service gives to your clients and how effectively you receive their incoming messages.

The telephone business is highly competitive, and there are many options to choose from. Explore them all, then choose those that suit both your budget and your business needs. Most phone companies offer calling features bundled together to give businesses plenty of options at competitive prices. Features to consider include call forwarding, call waiting, call display, and voice mail. Other considerations include long-distance calling and toll-free fax and phone service. Talk to or arrange a meeting with phone company sales representatives in your area. You will be able to choose from the many options available to small businesses today, which include the following.

Hands-free/speakerphone

The option of a speakerphone is great if you plan to have frequent meetings over the phone. It also allows you to do other work while on hold.

Cellular or mobile phone

Although airtime can be expensive, a mobile phone is an essential tool in running a special events business. This is a business where you will be on the go quite a bit, and being able to forward your business number to your cell phone can be very convenient if you are waiting for an important call. A mobile phone also makes it possible for clients to reach you on site at an event. Today's mobile packages have expanded to offer MP3 players, the ability to send pictures, and text messaging.

Hand-held wireless device or PDA

Hand-held wireless or mobile devices are quickly becoming the must-haves of those on the go, which includes people in the special events business. These devices range from the PDA, or personal digital assistant, to "smart phones" to wireless hand-held devices such as the Blackberry. The advantages to these devices are many, as they allow you to access a wide variety of business needs on the go, such as e-mail, phone services, an organizer, and calendar software. Depending on the provider and the device, many of the features can be integrated with your home office computer, such as entering tasks and accessing your calendar and contact lists. Currently, the technology that supports these options can be expensive. (Blackberry charges for e-mail volume.) As they gain popularity, access will become more affordable.

Voice over internet protocol

Another technological advance worth investigating is the voice over internet protocol, or VOIP: the ability to make telephone calls over the internet. In the business and traditional phone company world, this technology is still in its infancy. Although VOIP promises consumers a daring future that includes free local and long-distance calling, it is wise to proceed cautiously. Depending on the service provider, you may need to purchase an internet protocol (IP) phone or a special adapter to use your conventional telephone. Other special adapters allow you to transport your local number to anywhere with broadband internet access. This adapter is just a box that you bring with you when you travel. Just plug into the internet connection, plug in the phone, and voilà: free local calling.

Courier company

Shop around for the right courier company for your business. Compare rates and meet with a couple of them before deciding on which company's services you will choose. A reliable courier service with friendly staff is important to any business.

Company vehicle

Obviously, running a special events business will require you to be on the road a fair amount of time. Although there is no requirement to invest in a costly vehicle, you should have ready access to a reliable, presentable vehicle. Leasing is often a desirable option for those who depend on their vehicle for work. Talk to your local auto dealers and investigate options if you need to consider upgrading. You should try to estimate the amount of driving you will do to reach your clients, depending on the types of special events you plan to focus on. Weigh considerations such as fuel costs and in-vehicle space. Any charges incurred while using your own vehicle for company business can be used as tax deductions. (See chapter 11 for more on record keeping and taxes.)

Office Equipment and Setup

Taking the time to set up your office properly at the start will save you valuable time down the road. Consider your needs and make sure that your work space displays good ergonomics, promoting safety and efficiency. (Ergonomics, or human engineering, is the field that studies the relationship between people and their working environment.) Go to your local library or search the internet for resource material on setting up an ergonomically friendly work space. You may have office surplus suppliers in your area (including government operations), which offer good quality equipment at very good prices. Basic office equipment should cost anywhere from $500 for second-hand furnishings. Spend the money on a good comfortable chair as you will spend much time at your desk on the phone. If you can afford them, "extras" such as potted plants, artwork, and a coffee machine can help to make your environment more comfortable.

The basics you will need to set up your office consist of the following items:

- *Desk:* A large L-shaped desk is a good choice, offering enough space for your phone, computer, and some handy reference materials along with plenty of writing space.

- *Chair:* Purchase a good-quality office chair on casters with adjustable arms; your back will thank you for it.

- *Filing cabinet:* You will use this for customer files and company documents. One should be enough when starting your business. Invest in a good second-hand filing cabinet.

- *Bookcase:* You might also try shelving for storing large catalogues, stationery, etc.

- *Telephone:* As previously discussed, you may want to purchase a telephone with multi-line capabilities so you do not have to invest in new equipment when the time comes to add extra telephone lines. The cost of a multi-line telephone starts at about $200.

- *Guest chairs:* Also consider investing in a small meeting table with comfortable chairs.

Electronic Equipment

A computer with internet connectivity (cable or ADSL are your best bets), a printer, and a fax machine are essential tools for your business. Not only do they allow you to present a professional image, but they also enable you to communicate quickly and efficiently with your prospective clients. However, you can easily become overwhelmed trying to make your decisions when shopping for these items. The technology for electronic equipment is constantly changing.

Ask around for referrals to reputable dealers who offer training, will make service calls, and offer a phone-in help line. Do extensive research before committing to a system, and make sure that it is the right one for you and your type of operation.

Computer and printer

With the right computer and software, you will be able to efficiently do your bookkeeping and accounting, invoicing, payables, receivables, payroll, and marketing. You will also be able to update your customer database and generate professional quotes and correspondence. Dedicated software also allows you to set up your own website to give your company an online presence. See chapter 8 for more information on setting up a company website.

Prices for computer equipment can vary a great deal from one supplier to another. Purchasing this equipment can be a big investment, so keep in mind that prices change as quickly as technology. Do your homework, shop around, and compare prices. Choosing one supplier for all your equipment is the best way to ensure compatibility among components — and the best bet for receiving a discount. Most reputable sources will match the price of other dealers. You may also want to consider leasing computer equipment and paying for it over time.

Software for the events business

Once you have decided on your computer, your next big purchase to launch a special events business is dedicated software. Most personal computers these days come with the same standard software that businesses require to run their day-to-day operations. For the small business, of course, there are plenty of choices out there. The PC, which works with the Windows operating system, is commonplace among both business and home users. An alternative is to purchase a Macintosh computer running the Mac OS X operating system, which is PC compatible. This means that Mac users can easily open PC files on their computers and run many of the same programs, such as *Microsoft Office*, in a Mac version.

Microsoft Office is a great software product to keep your small business running efficiently and profitably. Often *Microsoft Office* will come already loaded on your new PC, although you should clarify whether it is a trial version that you will have to pay for separately later on. Most small businesses will find that this software is all they need to get started. With it, you can choose from an array of templates for letters and faxes; create a database for storing client information; develop professional-quality computer-generated slide presentations; and set up spreadsheets for managing budgets.

If you are unfamiliar with these products, speak to someone who works with these software packages and operating systems and ask to see the software in action. Have a list of questions ready that relate to what you want your software to accomplish. You will also want to ask about ways in which to protect your computer (and your client's computers!) from viruses that spread over the internet. Ask for recommendations on anti-virus software and firewall packages. (*Norton AntiVirus*, a Symantec product, is among the most popular.) Also ask about ways to install critical patches that prevent holes in your operating system from leaving you vulnerable to internet hackers.

There is also plenty of software specific to the special events/meeting planning industry. Good event software may cost about $350 and up, but in the long run it will save you valuable time and money. Let your software do some of the work for you by assisting you in the planning and organizing of your next event. Software is available for virtually all aspects of event planning, including speaker management, banquet seating, budgeting, scheduling, registration, surveys, fund-raising, and auctions.

Before you make a decision to purchase event software, you must be clear on the type of events or services for which your company will provide services. For example, you would not want to waste money on a meeting-room planner software if your company's specialty is golf tournaments. Always do a lot of research before purchasing specialized software. Ask to see a demo, and ask for a list of clients you can call before purchasing the software. Check out the competition. Question why one software is more expensive than another. Ask about training and whether there is a 24-hour customer service/help line.

Choosing industry-specific software may be overwhelming when you are just launching your business. If you find it so, just stick with a solid bundle, such as *Microsoft Office*, and build a wish list over a few months. A bit of on-the-ground experience will allow you to make a decision about what is important for you and your business to run effectively and efficiently.

Corbin Ball is a name to remember when it comes to special events software and technology. His website, <www.corbinball.com> provides comprehensive and up-to-date information on meeting planning and events technology online. Quite simply, you cannot find a better "one-stop" resource for information on event planning software. You can also find the link to "The Ultimate Technology Guide for Meeting Professionals" on the website, or just visit <www.mpifoundation.org>. There you can download the complimentary guide of more than 1,200 event/meeting industry-related software packages, from site selection to post-event analysis. These software solutions automate respective jobs, provide data analysis, increase accuracy, and streamline nearly every function of the business. The job directory is even classified into numerous categories; each listing includes pricing, contact information, web addresses, company history, and technical details.

Facsimile machine

Fax machines offer an efficient and economical way to communicate with clients, suppliers, and business associates. The fax machine allows you to send and receive documents for signing, such as registration forms, quotes, and contracts. It is less expensive than an elaborate telephone system, eliminates time spent on the telephone (which can tie up your line), and eliminates any verbal misunderstandings. Your fax machine can also serve as a photocopier in some cases, saving you the cost of buying a photocopier or paying a copying service.

If you have a computer with a modem, you can purchase software that will enable you to use your computer as a fax machine. If you decide on the fax-modem option, remember that while you can receive any kind of fax, you can only send information that is already on your computer. If you want to fax a brochure to a client, you will have to scan it into your computer before you can fax it using a fax-modem.

Digital camera and scanner

For today's special events business, a digital camera is an essential tool of the trade. Prices have dropped dramatically over the years, so it is wise to invest in a reliable, good-quality version for documenting your events and creating an e-mail portfolio or images to use on your website. Scanners can be equally useful in the business for promoting your business and communicating to clients. You will probably want to scan in photos, newspaper stories, and resource information from books and magazines.

Other equipment

For the special events company, there is no real need to invest in a photocopy machine. Many copying needs can be done either at your local copy shop or a custom printing shop. As mentioned, some fax machines are able to photocopy, and there are growing numbers of inexpensive, 24-hour photocopying outlets.

Office Supplies

In the special events business, you need very little in the way of office supplies to get you started. It is easy to get carried away by the many options available in paper stock, print quality, and general office supplies. This section covers the basics of what you need without spending more than you should.

Custom printing

Although software programs make it possible to print letterhead and other stationery using your own computer, utilizing the services of a custom printer will ensure that you have professional-quality business stationery. Get a few quotes from reputable printers in your area to find a good supplier. Ask to see samples and find out what savings you can achieve by using certain types of paper stock (matte versus glossy) and by limiting colors. More information on establishing a "visual identity" through the use of logos, etc., on your business stationery is included in chapter 8.

General office supplies

Before you launch your business, go to your local stationery store and stock up on general office supplies. You may be able to find better prices for these supplies at a big-box store, and some also offer free delivery. The last thing you will want to be doing once you are in business is using valuable work time to purchase the little things for your office. Here is a list of the office supplies you will need to get going:

- Pens and pencils
- Markers
- Post-it notes
- Writing pads
- Computer and fax machine supplies: paper, print cartridges, etc.
- Plain and mailing envelopes
- File folders
- Binders
- Tape
- Scissors
- Stapler and staples
- Three-hole punch
- Paper clips
- Wall and or desk calendar
- Appointment book

Plan on budgeting $200 to $300 for start-up office supplies. See Sample 1 for an example of what your initial estimates and start-up cost analysis might look like.

BUSINESS START-UP COSTS

Purchases for:	Studio/Office	Home-based
Office furniture	$500	$500
Telephone	150	150
Answering machine	75	75
Computer and printer	3,500	3,500
Computer software	500	500
Fax machine	600	600
Storage shelves	200	200
Graphic design services	1,000	500
Brochures*	3,000	1,000
Initial stationery and business cards	750	250
Initial opening inventory	2,500	1,500
Office supplies	300	300
Legal	800	800
Accounting set-up	500	500
Rent security deposit	500	0
TOTAL	**$14,875**	**$10,375**

Home-based is estimated on $125,000 in revenue

Studio/office space is based on $250,000 in revenue.

* Brochure costs based on

    2,000 three-panel, 8" x 11" brochures

    Studio: four-color

    Home-based: two-color

4
Financial Planning and Management

Careful financial planning is crucial when establishing a new business venture, not only in the start-up stage as discussed in chapter 3, but continually once your business is established. Planning or forecasting your revenues and expenses may seem like an impossible challenge for the new business owner because there is no financial history to base your forecast on, but it can and must be done. You need to have two simple issues in mind as you start your new venture: what the costs are and what revenues you can expect from your business. This chapter discusses some reasons for forecasting sales and expenses for your new venture.

Financing Your Venture

Most business funding comes from a combination of personal savings, family and friends, financial institutions, business partners, and private investors. Before you think about borrowing money, keep in mind the risks involved. As a small-business owner, you should always feel a little bit uneasy about debt and work hard to keep it under control. If it is necessary to borrow money, borrow only what you need and only when you need it. Following are several options for financing your business venture.

Personal savings

The ideal situation for starting a new business is financing it yourself. If you have the personal resources to run your business until it returns a profit, you will have no lenders to answer to, no bank interest to pay, and no financial responsibilities other than to yourself and your company. There is no better or less stressful way to start a new enterprise than debt free.

If the financial demands of your new business are small, you might want to consider waiting until you have the savings to independently finance your venture. If you are starting a larger venture that needs more initial capital, it will still be necessary to show potential lenders and investors that you have something more to invest than just your ideas and time.

Family and friends

Many small-business ventures start with the generosity of family and friends. Most often this type of financing takes the form of a loan on trust, accepted in good faith, with no collateral required. There is always a danger in mixing business financing with personal relationships, so this option should be approached with careful consideration; the terms and conditions of the loan should be reasonable and negotiated in a businesslike manner. Have a lawyer prepare a legal promissory note that outlines all the terms and conditions.

Most important, be certain you will be able to pay the money back on time and in full. Before accepting the loan, think about a backup payment plan should the business be unable to repay the debt.

Financial institutions

The most logical approach to securing a loan from a financial institution is to select one where you already have a history of responsible financial dealings and an already established relationship with the manager or loans officer.

Be well prepared when you approach any potential lender. Have a clear, concise, typed, well-presented business plan. Present the lender with your sales and cash flow projections, and explain precisely how much money you want to borrow and why. Be very specific and show how your business can be expected to generate the cash to repay the loan.

Be prepared to show statements of your personal net worth and what other financial resources you have available to start up your business. If you want to win the confidence of the bank manager or loans officer, be prepared to answer all questions truthfully and candidly.

It is unlikely that you will be able to secure a bank loan unless you have some tangible assets as security. If you own a home and are willing to mortgage it, or mortgage it further, a lender is more likely to make funds available.

When you borrow money for your new business, you are personally liable to pay it back. Even if your company is incorporated, the lender will require a personal guarantee from you. If a bank or credit union agrees to grant you a loan, it will usually require you to take out property and liability insurance on your business and a life insurance policy on yourself, naming the bank as beneficiary.

A financial institution may come up with a variety of reasons for turning down your request for a loan. If you do not succeed at the first lender you try, go to others. Ask why you are being turned down for financing and make adjustments accordingly. Perhaps you need to revamp your business plan or start your business on a smaller scale. You may also want to consider taking out a personal loan. This is sometimes the easiest method for many small-business entrepreneurs to secure financing, especially when the amount needed for start-up is small. To receive a personal loan, you will still need to have collateral and satisfy the bank of your ability to pay. However, you will not need to provide the bank with a business plan or to go into the details of your proposed venture.

Private investors

Going into business with someone you know can be difficult; starting a business with someone you don't know can be impossible and usually comes with stringent conditions. The best source for finding private investors is your accountant. People with money to invest in small start-up ventures often rely on their accountants for advice.

Expect such investors to be cautious and to attach conditions to the loan. Their approach to lending money to a small business is similar to that of a bank, and you will need to provide them with the same type of information you would provide to a loan officer with any financial institution. Note that private investors seldom invest in a small-business venture unless there is a possibility of a greater than average return on investment.

Government

The governments of both the United States and Canada provide financial assistance to small business.

In the United States, the Small Business Administration (SBA) exists to help small business educationally and financially. You should check your phone book for the office nearest you and see a counselor for current information on funding. You can also call the SBA's Small Business Answer Desk at 1-800-827-5722.

In Canada, money for small business comes from a variety of government departments both provincial and federal. Check the small-business development department of your provincial government.

It should be noted that most government lending is done as "last resort" lending. It often takes the form of loan guarantees rather than direct loans. You may have to prove you were unable to obtain money from other sources. Generally, the government will expect that you have some of your own money invested in the enterprise. There may also be restrictions on the type of businesses that receive funding. Learn what programs are available through the various levels of government.

Before approaching any government lending department for funds, prepare proper documentation on your business. The rules of preparation and professionalism apply any time you seek either commercial or government financial assistance.

Many government programs give loans or loan guarantees to incorporated businesses only. Small proprietorships often find themselves ineligible for certain types of government funding. Even if you do strike out, the process of learning what is available is worthwhile. You may not be eligible now, but there may be a time later in your business cycle when your business will qualify, and the time spent will not have been wasted.

Your Business Plan

A good business plan is a simple, honest document that completely and precisely describes your experience, your proposed business, and your long-term plans for that business. It does not need to be long or complicated; it should tell a complete story that can be easily understood by a potential lender or investor.

A business plan is expected to follow a standard format, but it should be tailored to suit the situation. How your business plan is presented is as important as the information it contains. For professional polish, use a 12-point font for the text, double-spaced and printed on standard white paper. Have someone else proofread it and make sure it contains no mistakes or spelling and grammatical errors.

It should have a separate cover page with the company name, address, telephone and fax numbers, and your name as the person to contact for further information. It should also show the date that the document was prepared. Each section of the plan should have a heading and the pages should be numbered.

You might want to consider writing a short cover letter offering to provide any additional information that might be required. If you write a cover letter, make sure you have the correct information for your contact.

A business plan that includes three or four pages of solid information and a cash flow forecast will probably be sufficient for starting up a small special events business. If you have done thorough market research and financial forecasts, you will have all the information necessary to write a business plan.

Following is a brief discussion of each of the components that go into a business plan.

Executive summary

Your business plan should outline the following essential facts regarding your proposed business:

(a) Type of business

(b) Location of the business

(c) Legal structure of the business (proprietorship, partnership, incorporated company)

(d) Names of any other shareholders

(e) The amount of funds required

(f) The terms under which those funds will be repaid

Personal experience and background

This section includes your up-to-date resume and those of any partners or other key people in your proposed venture. Emphasize why your background and experience or that of your partner or key personnel is valuable to the success of your business. Potential lenders or investors must feel that you have the experience and expertise to make your business work. They are very aware that mismanagement can be a cause of business failure.

Description of service

Describe your special events business and service clearly and concisely. Explain why there is a need for your service and why it will do well in your chosen market. Emphasize the strengths your service has over your competition. Make sure you highlight your service's uniqueness. Emphasize that your business will be home-based or in low-cost office space with low overhead, which will allow you to sell your service at a reasonable price.

Sales and marketing strategy

Prove that you have done your market research by providing details on your potential clients and how you intend to reach them. Explain how you will use the information you have gathered as the basis of your sales and marketing strategy. Describe your competition and why your service will sell in your targeted market. Show that you have a good understanding of your chosen market and why a potential lender should feel confident that your sales and marketing planning will be successful. See chapter 8 for more information on sales and marketing.

Forecasts and projections

This section of your business plan should be a summary of fixed expenses and overhead, planned sales and marketing expenses, start-up costs, projected revenue forecast, and a projected cash flow analysis. Your cash flow forecast should be a truthful and realistic projection of the financial needs of your new business. It should show the potential lender that the business has the ability to pay back the amount borrowed. This is generally where most lenders will be looking for weaknesses in your plan, so be prepared for scrutiny and to answer any questions regarding your proposed business.

For more detailed advice on business plans, consult *Preparing a Successful Business Plan*, another title in the Self-Counsel Business Series.

Financial Management

If you begin with a good business plan, you are off to a good start in your business's financial management. Sound planning encourages you to think practically about the factors critical to your business, such as costs, space requirements, equipment purchases, and so on. The following list outlines some key benefits provided by a detailed business plan:

(a) Allows you to see your business on paper before you invest any money

(b) Indicates at what point your venture will break even and begin to show a profit

(c) Helps a lender or investor see the merits and potential profitability of your business

(d) Prepares you for the possible risks of starting a business and guides you in your personal financial planning

(e) Tells you how long your start-up capital will last and at what point you will need to rely on the revenues to operate the business

In addition, to prepare a financial forecast — an important part of a business plan — you must know and be able to predict the following:

(a) What is the amount of cash on hand you have to invest in your new business?

(b) What amount of loans or borrowed money from outside sources is available?

(c) What is your business capacity? How many events can you realistically expect to produce per year?

(d) What will you charge for your services?

(e) Based on your sales and marketing efforts, how many special events and what types of events can you produce?

(f) What are the costs involved in producing events?

(g) What are the fixed expenses of running your business?

Forecasting cash flow

Understanding cash flow is an absolute necessity for the new business owner. Along with loans and your personal investment, the cash flow into your business is created by the number of events you are paid to produce. The amount of cash your business will earn will depend on the number of events you produce and the income generated by producing those events.

In chapter 5, we discuss setting a price for your events and services. The cash flow out of your business is linked to the costs of producing your events and the expenses of running your business. Naturally, as a viable business, your objective should be to bring in more cash than goes out. To plan and monitor that process you need to develop a cash flow forecast. This forecast requires that you take into account fixed expenses and overhead, marketing costs, and start-up costs. You also need to forecast revenues. The next sections look at these elements in turn.

Fixed expenses and overhead

Fixed expenses and overhead are the costs incurred in running your business and are constant regardless of how many events you produce. Make a list of all the expenses that will be paid by your company and whether they are monthly, quarterly, or annual expenses.

See Sample 2 for an example of overhead expenses that could be incurred by a special events company.

Worksheet 2 is for you to figure out your own expenses. When making your own list, eliminate items that do not apply to your operation and add any that are missing.

Marketing costs

In addition to your fixed costs and the costs of producing an event, there are costs incurred in marketing your services. In order to do a cash flow, you must have a marketing plan and forecast a budget for your first year of operation. Included in your marketing plan should be the expenses listed in Worksheet 3. See chapter 8 for more information on what goes into marketing.

OVERHEAD AND FIXED EXPENSES

Studio/office:	Monthly	Quarterly	Annually
Advertising	$790	$2,370	$9,480
Rent	500	1,500	6,000
Telephone line	60	180	720
Fax line	60	180	720
Utilities	50	150	600
Gas	100	300	1,200
Office supplies	50	150	600
Postage	25	75	300
Photocopies	20	60	240
Courier charges	20	60	240
Dues and memberships	50	150	600
Travel	25	75	300
Licenses			100
Insurance	75	225	900
Accounting			1,000
Legal			300
Health plan	40	120	480
Wages and benefits	1,000	3,000	12,000
Interest and bank charges	20	60	240
TOTAL	**$2,885**	**$8,655**	**$36,020**

Home-based:			
Advertising	$275	$825	$3,300
Telephone/fax	60	180	720
Utilities	33	100	400
Gas	100	300	1,200
Office supplies	50	150	600
Postage	25	75	300
Photocopies	20	60	240
Courier charges	10	30	120
Dues and memberships	50	150	600
Travel	25	75	300
Licenses			100
Insurance	75		900
Accounting		250	1,000
Legal			300
Interest and bank charge	20	60	240
TOTAL	**$743**	**$2,255**	**$10,270**

WORKSHEET 2
BUSINESS EXPENSES

Expense	$ Amount		
	Monthly	**Quarterly**	**Annually**
Advertising	_____	_____	_____
Rent	_____	_____	_____
Telephone line	_____	_____	_____
Fax line	_____	_____	_____
Yellow Pages listing	_____	_____	_____
Utilities	_____	_____	_____
Automobile	_____	_____	_____
Office supplies	_____	_____	_____
Postage	_____	_____	_____
Photocopies	_____	_____	_____
Shipping	_____	_____	_____
Courier charges	_____	_____	_____
Dues and memberships	_____	_____	_____
Travel	_____	_____	_____
Licenses	_____	_____	_____
Insurance	_____	_____	_____
Accounting	_____	_____	_____
Legal	_____	_____	_____
Health plan	_____	_____	_____
Equipment rental	_____	_____	_____
Wages and benefits	_____	_____	_____
Interest and bank charges	_____	_____	_____

WORKSHEET 3
MARKETING EXPENSES

Item	$ Amount		
	Monthly	**Quarterly**	**Annually**
Print advertising	_____	_____	_____
Web advertising	_____	_____	_____
Yellow Pages	_____	_____	_____
Direct mail	_____	_____	_____
Trade shows	_____	_____	_____
Special events	_____	_____	_____
Promotions	_____	_____	_____
Other	_____	_____	_____
Other	_____	_____	_____
Other	_____	_____	_____
Other	_____	_____	_____
Other	_____	_____	_____

Start-up costs

Start-up costs include your purchases for all the equipment, furniture, and sales materials necessary to start your new venture. Worksheet 4 lists of some of the start-up expenses that might be incurred by a new special events company. Eliminate those that do not apply to your operation and add any that are missing to work out your start-up expenses.

Forecasting revenues

Forecasting the revenue you will bring in during your first year of operation is one of the most difficult steps in preparing your cash flow projections and business plan. Review your market research materials and estimate how many clients you can hope to attract each month. Be realistic and take into consideration how many events you alone can produce in a day, a week, a month.

Also consider the amount of time necessary to get your marketing materials into circulation to build a customer base. Prepare a chart of the revenues you anticipate each month for a year. Consider planned vacations and other personal commitments. Do several different versions, including the least amount of revenue generated or client events you will require each month to reach a break-even point after your fixed expenses. See Worksheet 5 for an outline of monthly revenue forecasts.

At this point you should have all the information you need on the fixed expenses and overhead, start-up costs, and projected revenues for one year. Now you are ready to prepare a cash flow forecast. You can do this manually using a standard 13-column accounting pad or on your computer if you prefer, using spreadsheet software.

To prepare a basic cash flow forecast, you will need a list of your expenses, broken down monthly, quarterly and annually as in Sample 2. This is your comprehensive list of all outgoing monies for overhead and fixed expenses, which includes business expenses, marketing expenses, and interest and bank charges for start-up costs (Worksheet 2 and Sample 2). You will also need your forecasted monthly revenues (Worksheet 5). The cash flow breaks down the expenses by month and charts your total cash (revenues + any other income dedicated to your special events business) at the start of each month. The formula is basically —

revenues – expenses = cash flow

START-UP EXPENSES

Purchase	$ Amount
Office furniture	_____
Telephone	_____
Answering machine	_____
Computer and printer	_____
Computer software	_____
Fax machine	_____
Portfolio	_____
Storage shelves	_____
Graphic design services	_____
Brochure printing	_____
Initial supply stationery and business cards	_____
Business License	_____
Legal incorporation or name registration	_____

WORKSHEET 5
MONTHLY REVENUE FORECAST

Month		$ Total
January	_____	_____
February	_____	_____
March	_____	_____
April	_____	_____
May	_____	_____
June	_____	_____
July	_____	_____
August	_____	_____
September	_____	_____
October	_____	_____
November	_____	_____
December	_____	_____

Your cash flow forecast will act as your guide by keeping you to a budget that shows you on paper when you are on or off your plan. It will be difficult to be absolute in your first forecasting efforts. Remember, these are projections, not bookkeeping exercises. You will have to make certain assumptions in the beginning, especially when it comes to preparing your projected revenues. However, by trying to be as accurate as possible when it comes to expenses, you will have a clearer idea of the kind of revenues you will need to produce in order to pay yourself an income and potentially break even.

There are many terrific sources for more information on preparing financial forecasts. Banks often have good information at both their physical and online locations, and government departments do as well. Visit the United States Small Business Association at <www.sba.gov/financing/index.html> or the Canadian federal government Business Start-Up Assistant site at <bsa.cbsc.org/gol/bsa/interface.nsf/engdoc/0.html> on the internet. As mentioned earlier, you may also wish to acquire *Preparing a Successful Business Plan*, another title in the Self-Counsel Press Business Series.

Either way, it is absolutely necessary for the ongoing success of your business to prepare these financial forecasts now and on an ongoing basis as your business grows and prospers. Good financial management helps you control your business and plan for success.

5
Pricing Your Services

Establishing a fee for your services can be one of the most difficult tasks when setting up a small business. As there are so many variables to consider, it is far more difficult to set a fee for service than it is to establish the cost of a product. The type of special events business you plan on operating will factor into this decision as well. However, the decision-making process for setting your prices will follow a common formula. This formula means that you need to be fully aware of your event production costs. Whatever method you choose, it is critical that you establish pricing at the outset. The following sections discuss various options to consider when you are establishing your business rates.

Competitive Pricing

Knowing what your competition is charging is a good idea when you are in business for yourself. However, do not make the mistake of setting your prices based on what others charge. It is critical that you do a sound analysis of your market's needs and your financial needs based on your expenses and overhead. When setting your price, it is important that you don't price yourself out of a project with fees that are too high — or give the impression you provide less than quality service by charging fees that are too low. Usually, those starting out in the business will charge lower prices, but if you have years of experience working for someone else, your fees should reflect this.

Certainly, as a small business with lower overhead you should pass savings along to your customer, but if you are planning and executing large events, you will need to ensure that all your costs (overhead and production costs) are covered in order to stay in business.

Hourly Fee and Daily Rates

Charging an hourly fee is a common method used by special events planners, especially those working as special events consultants. Hourly rates for consultants can range from low-end fees of about $25 per hour to more than $100 per hour charged by high-end contractors. Experienced consultants often quote a daily rate in addition to an hourly fee. This type of rate gives the client the opportunity to have an event consultant available for long hours at one cost, unlike a simple hourly rate arrangement in which any downtime between events is charged at full cost.

Even if you are just starting out, as already mentioned, it is often a good idea to charge a mid-level rate to give the impression of value to your clients. Some corporate clients would never consider hiring someone who charged less than $45 an hour, for there is a perceived lack of quality associated with a lower price.

To provide a quote based on hourly rates, you need to be able to accurately gauge the amount of time a project will take and what costs you will incur in delivering the service. You will also need to ensure that you are not expected to incur extra costs in your rate, such as rentals, food and beverage services, supplies, and staffing. If you are, those costs should be charged back to the client directly at cost. Otherwise, you would be better off using another method of pricing alone or in combination with your hourly rate.

Cost-Plus Pricing

Pricing on a cost-plus basis involves setting a profit margin on the cost of an event. Depending on the costs associated with a particular event (i.e., the production costs of services and materials involved, salary, and overhead), your profit margin could range anywhere between 10 percent and 25 percent. It is critical that you factor in all the costs of an event to establish a profit; if your fee is dependent on ticket sales from an event, you must also establish a minimum fee.

As an example, let us assume that you are organizing and producing an awards banquet in the ballroom of a hotel. Your client has a budget of $50,000 for this event. To earn a profit of 10 percent, which is $5,000, you need to keep your costs to $45,000. In producing an event of this kind, your costs will include at minimum the following: venue cost, catering (potentially bar and beverage), staffing, décor, staging, audiovisual, entertainment, the award itself, insurance, and contingencies as well as any service charges, licensing fees, and taxes required.

Drawbacks to this type of pricing include customer concerns that consultants who earn a percentage of an overall budget are less inclined to look for cost efficiencies. Another drawback is ensuring that your time is compensated if you are referred from one customer at a specific percentage to another with a more complicated event and a smaller budget. Additionally, clients producing events with very high budgets will expect you to take a smaller profit. For large events, often a flat fee and cost-plus pricing is the preferred method of billing.

Flat Fee

Many of the considerations for cost-plus pricing apply to the charging of flat fees. You will need to be able to effectively ascertain the costs involved in producing an event and know what you need to take away in order to make a profit. In the beginning, estimating these costs will be time-consuming and demanding, and you may find yourself out of pocket somewhat. However, as you gain experience and establish resources, estimating costs will become second nature.

Some clients will have set expectations as to what the consultation fee should be when you quote on a job. To address this, it is always a good idea to show that you are flexible and willing to work with their needs to establish a firm price.

Often, corporate clients or those who produce many events may have their own resources or can recommend suppliers where they receive discounts, which can save on costs you incur in producing their events. Don't be afraid to ask for specifics when giving quotes.

Commission

Commission on producing an event may be charged on events where you are involved in ticket sales, exhibit booth space, or registration of participants. However, unless you are very experienced in sales and marketing or the event has a solid track record of sales, working on straight commission is no guarantee that you will make a profit for your services.

Discounting

You need to be as careful about how you discount as you are about how you charge. Be absolutely clear about when and why you discount. The business world is small, and you don't want to confuse your clients or establish the wrong impression in your market by frequently changing the way you charge. Indeed, it can be very tricky to offer discounts, but there are a number of situations when you might want to consider offering lower prices. These circumstances include the following:

Fund-raiser events

For those just starting out, fund-raiser events offer good exposure for your business as well as experience to offer to future clients. It is common practice to offer non-profit organizations a discount on fees in the range of 10 percent to 25 percent. In exchange, these organizations will usually list your business as a sponsor or as a contributor to the success of the fund-raiser through various means of communication. See chapter 8 for more information on advertising and promotion.

Suppliers

Sometimes you might be asked to provide event services to one of your suppliers or to one of the companies you work with. Some special events businesses choose to offer a discount in exchange for a reduced fee or waived fee on future orders or business. However, proceed carefully in this regard, as event (and other) businesses can sometimes encounter negative reactions from clients who decide, legitimately or not, that these event businesses choose to work with suppliers that discount so they can receive higher profits. Although this may be true in some situations, the fact is that long-established connections with suppliers can lead to discounted prices, and event businesses work with these suppliers because they know them to be reliable and provide quality supplies.

6
Client and Supplier Contracts: Protecting Your Business

A contract is a formal agreement, usually a written agreement. If everything in business always went well, we wouldn't need written contracts. Sometimes having a written contract can help the parties to that contract resolve basic misunderstandings that may have occurred between them. Often, the only time a written contract is studied intensely is when things go sour, and the contract has the answers regarding the rights of the parties.

There are two main types of contracts you will be involved with in the special events business. One is the master contract between you and a client who has hired you to work on an event. The other is the contract between you and any business that will provide the necessary supplies for the event. Usually, the supplier contracts will be arranged by you; however, there will be occasions on which contracts are held between your client and the supplier. Bear in mind that having your own contracts with suppliers increases your control, but it also increases your risk.

Supplier Contracts

Your suppliers, such as hotels, bands, décor companies, etc., will likely have their own standard contract. Having a standard form contract, however, does not mean you should not analyze it carefully. When a contract contains a lot of fine print, there is a tendency to skip over the details as they are seen as too boring or too difficult to read. There is also a tendency to assume that the fine print must be standard, and that it is accepted by all who deal with that particular supplier. You need to be aware that important clauses are often hidden in the fine print just for that reason.

Here are some tips for dealing with the fine print. First, it does not need to remain fine print: increase the print size using the enlarge feature on most photocopy machines, until you find the print easy to read. Second, review only a few paragraphs of fine print at a time, even if it takes you several hours or even days to finish your review of the contract. Third, make sure you understand every paragraph before moving on. A contract is not like reading a novel: it is not enough to understand just the general idea of the paragraph. In a contract, you must understand the specific meaning of each sentence. If a paragraph is not clear, ask your lawyer to explain it to you. Don't ask the supplier who sent you the contract, because you won't necessarily receive a correct or even a straight answer. And last, you should never feel embarrassed about asking a supplier to attach an addendum to his or her contract that uses plain English to describe some matter that is not clear to you in the fine print.

Client Contracts

You should have your own form of contract with your client. A pre-prepared printed contract form always looks more professional. Of course, no single form of contract can cover all the provisions applicable to a range of special events. Therefore, your standard contract should be designed so that schedules or other attachments can be added.

To draft a comprehensive contract, you will most likely need the services of a lawyer. However, you can save on the costs of a lawyer by doing your homework before hiring one. Start by making a list, in point form, of all the different matters that you think should be in your standard form contract. Restrict yourself to one thought per point, and do not waste time trying to use legal language in summarizing your point. Add your ideas as to how you are, or should be, protected against such problems. In the special events business, much thought must be given to the so-called "attrition" clauses, which deal with what happens when an event needs to be modified or even cancelled if the projected number of attendees is significantly reduced. The specifics of attrition must be set out through a formula or sliding scale that is applied to any number of attendees.

Send your list of points to your lawyer to prepare a first draft of your standard form contract for the client. As you've already done the homework described above, you will have saved time — billable time — that might otherwise have been spent by your lawyer having to extract this same detail from you at an initial meeting.

While having your own client contract is best, corporate or government clients will often have legal contracts that are used with all outsourced services. In some cases, a contract may be referred to as a services agreement or letter of intent, but it is still a legally binding agreement to fulfill a service. As with supplier contracts, you will want to be absolutely clear on every term and condition set out — you need to ensure that there are no legal loopholes that could leave you burdened with unexpected costs or obligations.

Contract Finalization

Having created your standard form contract or having fully reviewed a supplier's contract, you should ensure your efforts are not wasted as a result of failure to finalize a contract properly.

See Sample 3, for a checklist to help prepare you while you become accustomed to working with different clients and suppliers and their contracts or services agreements.

SAMPLE 3
CONTRACT CHECKLIST: SAFEGUARDING YOUR BUSINESS

To cover the basics of every contract, always:

- ensure the contract is dated;

- ensure that the other party to the contract is properly identified by legal name and description (e.g., if your client is a corporation, verify the corporation's correct or legal name, and check that the corporation is valid);

- ensure that an authorized contact is provided (name and any contact information like phone, fax, and e-mail) for dispute resolution and any negotiations or amendments required;

- include your company's legal name and address;

- spell out the details: include the event name and proposed timelines and a description of the event;

- include the scope of services to be provided with as many details as possible and any goods or services to be provided by the other party;

- identify any subcontractors to be used or any services that will be contracted out;

- identify the activities that will require liability insurance, permits or licenses and clearly identify who is responsible for securing these;

- ensure that all copyright or ownership and any non-disclosure or confidentiality issues applicable are understood and accounted for;

- ensure that contract amount and/or payment terms are clearly specified and understood as to dates of payment and how additional goods, services, and expenses will be dealt with;

- ensure that cancellation or termination policies are set out clearly for both parties;

- try to have the other party sign the contract first; this keeps you from being left in limbo with a contract signed by you in the other party's hands while you have nothing in yours;

- document the expected return of the contract to you for signing; resist the temptation of starting work or making commitments in expectation that the signed contract will eventually show up;

- ensure that all attachments/schedules to the contract are, in fact, attached, and initial every page of the whole contract and any attachments before giving a signed copy back to the other party; and

- ensure that any changes or amendments to the contract are signed by each party.

7
Keeping Your Operations in Order

Striking a Balance

Most new special event companies are one-person operations. Be prepared to put in long hours when starting out. You will likely put in 50 to 60 hours each week if you are starting up a full-time business. You will be doing everything from cold-calling potential clients and attending functions to promote your business to routine business tasks such as keeping records and collecting payment.

It is easy in a business to spend all your time on the creative end at the expense of record keeping. You can't afford to let those details get out of hand; you need to know whether you are making or losing money. However, don't forget that you also need to be out marketing, advertising, and selling, not behind your computer all day figuring out detailed financial projections. You need to strike a balance to keep your business running smoothly and profitably.

Maintaining Financial Records

When you are starting out, you will likely generate different types of payment for your services. Remember, this is a business that requires you to keep track of other people's details; don't forget to keep track of yours. Among the details you need to stay on top of are accounts payable and accounts receivable. These will vary with each business and, in fact, with each event. So start off on a solid footing with a system that offers a place for everything and everything in its place. Build yourself a reminder system for both the bills you have to pay and the payments you are billing. Here are some suggestions to help you keep your financial records in order.

Set up a calendar and reminder system

Important dates and deadlines should be entered into an effective calendar system. (See the section on time management and setting priorities later in this chapter.) An effective calendar system will provide adequate lead time on various activities and prompt followup to ensure that all the tasks have been performed. One of the most common problems encountered in the special events business is losing track of billing dates, payments, and paperwork. Today, with all the software programs available, there are many excellent sources that will keep you on task and meeting deadlines. See chapter 3 for more on programs that combine project management with contact or database management systems.

Establish an efficient filing system

Take the time to develop an effective filing system to eliminate the possibility of misplacing supplier information or invoices. Your filing system should be designed so you can easily retrieve information on a client or a project when needed. Although much of your business information may be stored on your computer, good record keeping will still be necessary to manage paperwork that can't or shouldn't be entered into a computer system.

Keep separate files on each client. Keep your project expenses separate from your own expenses (e.g., overhead). File information as soon as you get it. Do not fall into the bad habit of letting paper pile up. Establish one day a month to process your accounts payable and try hard to keep to that date or close to it.

Good systems for filing abound, and you will develop your own as you go along. But when you start out, ensure that you have an efficient filing system in place that you can understand. Poor filing not only puts you behind in time, but it can also cost you losses in business. It can also get you in hot water if your business gets audited by the IRS (United States) or Canada Revenue Agency and you do not have your documents and records in order. For special events businesses in the United States, the IRS has good information on record keeping at <www.irs.gov/businesses/small/article /0,,id=99930,00.html> on the internet. In Canada, you will want to go to <www.cra-arc.gc.ca/E/pub/tg/rc4070/rc4070eq-01.html> for information from Canada Revenue Agency.

For more information, go to chapter 11, Accounting, Record Keeping, and Taxes.

Keep track of deposits

In the event business, it is common to receive a deposit prior to beginning the work. A deposit may be anywhere from 10 percent to 50 percent, with the balance payable at the completion of services. Make sure that you take note of the amount of the deposit so that you do not make the mistake of charging for the full amount at the end of the contract.

Keep track of retainers

Many larger companies prefer to hire special events businesses on a retainer basis. This type of payment will provide you with a specific amount of money over a specific amount of time. Depending on the client's preference, you may be required to submit statements on a regular basis detailing the work that has been done to date. Make sure you remember those dates, for missing them could mean the end of the contract.

Keep invoicing on track

In some cases, you may be under contract for a long-term project by a large corporation or government department, in which case it is not uncommon to be paid by project through the submission of a work order.

However, in most cases, you will be expected to submit an invoice. Most businesses issue checks on a regular schedule, often twice a month, or every 30 days. If you want to deal with that type of client (and you most definitely do), you must be prepared to invoice them and wait for payment.

When invoicing a client, you should always put the terms of payment on the invoice. Normally these terms would be payable on receipt of invoice and payable net 10 (or 15 or 30) days, depending on the terms you have negotiated with your client. If the accounts clerk at the company you are billing sees this on an invoice, he or she is more likely to issue you a payment during the next check run. See Sample 4 for an example of an invoice.

Establish regular billing, credit, and collection

As mentioned previously, you need to keep on top of your billing and invoicing. Monthly or interim billing should be done wherever possible if your clients are not paying immediately. This means bills can be sent close to the time the work was done. Regular billing keeps your cash flow even and enables you to spot any discrepancies. An effective record keeping system for credit and collection is also needed. Always double-check the invoices you receive from suppliers against original estimates.

Keep good tax records

Tax records record details of sales taxes, income taxes, business taxes, and employee income tax deductions. Most businesses are regulated by a combination of federal, state/provincial, and local governments. The information for these records is obtained from different aspects of the business operation. For example, payroll deductions are obtained from the payroll records, and information on goods and services taxes is collected from your monthly books. Ask your accountant for advice on tax matters.

Hire a professional bookkeeper and accountant

When you are starting out, you will be taking on the full load, but if you have a weakness in the financing and bookkeeping area, don't be afraid to hire a professional. Bookkeepers provide excellent services and keep many businesses afloat. They usually charge reasonable fees and come in very handy at tax time. Check out other small ventures to see if you can get a referral to a good one.

Chartered or Certified Accountants offer more detailed services than bookkeepers and will be able to provide you with the best advice on how to maximize write-offs and minimize expenses. They will also be versed in tax law and know the deadlines for filing business tax returns. However, accountants do not come cheap. We suggest

XYZ EVENTS

INVOICE

TO: Patricia Cohen
Marketing Associate
ABC Corporation
Suite 404, 908 Business Street
Vancouver, BC V6B 2M1

DATE: August 30, 2004

INVOICE#: 614

SUBJECT: ABC CORPORATE CHALLENGE — Event Management Services

Event Management Fee $ 10,000.00

GST #R000000000   700.00

TOTAL MANAGEMENT FEE $ 10,700.00

TERMS: Full amount owing is due upon receipt of invoice.

Thank you for giving XYZ Events the opportunity to work
with ABC on another successful CORPORATE CHALLENGE

1857 EVENTS AVENUE, VANCOUVER, BC V6J 1M4 • TEL: (604) 000-0000 • FAX: (604) 000-0001

you establish a relationship with a good accountant, but the monthly services of a bookkeeper will keep you in order so that at tax time, you can easily hand over an organized set of books and receipts, saving you much time and money.

Keeping Your Non-Financial Records in Order

All of your day-to-day operations, as discussed in this chapter, will generate a lot of paperwork that will need to be organized and that must be maintained. Just as you don't want the paperwork to overwhelm you, you also don't want to forget about it completely. Keeping good administrative records can improve your business's efficiency and profit. Non-financial records and office systems should be maintained carefully and updated consistently. Office systems should be implemented to reduce exposure to liability and to increase your awareness of how well the business is running.

Personnel records

If you hire casual help, or if your business grows to the point that you hire a regular employee, you will need to keep personnel records. These contain all documents and correspondence relating to an employee from the time he or she applies for employment to termination. Individual employee records also include a summary of personal data, education and training, work history, and job and wage record.

Research files

You will want to keep all your market research information filed for future use, but there are restrictions on what type of information you can keep. In 2004, the Government of Canada introduced legislation called the Personal Information Protection and Electronic Documents Act (PIPEDA), which governs commercial organizations' obligations with respect to personal information. Before you start keeping records on people you want as clients, go to <privacyforbusiness.ic.gc.ca/epic/internet/inpfb-cee.nsf/en/Home> to ensure that you are not contravening the laws that govern that information.

Managing Your Time

Time management is an essential skill in the special events business. Sensible time management begins by setting priorities, which will affect all aspects of your business.

The first year of your business is a busy one. You are required to take many steps on the way to your success. As you begin to produce special events, deal with suppliers, keep books and records, and so on, demands for your time will escalate.

It's a good idea to organize your agenda from the very beginning. We find it helps to divide your time into three segments: long-term, intermediate, and immediate. Define each segment of time in whatever way you like. For example, your long-term agenda could be a year, or it could be six months if you find that the time frame works better for you.

Long-term agenda

The foundation of time management is list-making, the act of setting down what you are going to do and when you plan to do it. Begin by deciding how long your long-term will be, then make a list of activities you must do in that time period.

You will find that assigning priority to the activities takes some thought, and it is easier to list what has to be done first and worry about ranking later. The main purpose of your agenda is to consider every possibility. Make your list as complete as you can.

Intermediate agenda

Your long-term agenda will likely run to more than one page if it is as complete as it should be. You begin to refine your agenda when you reach those items in the intermediate section. Start by reviewing every item on the long-term list. If you have chosen six months as your intermediate period, transfer all the things that need to be accomplished in this time frame to a new list.

Immediate agenda

Now you can create your immediate agenda. Follow the same procedure you used for your intermediate agenda. Scan your list and transfer all activities that require prompt attention to your new list.

If you have designated one week as the time period of your immediate agenda, look for dates that fall within that period. Write all the activities for that time span on the new list. Enter them by order of date.

If you wish, you can bypass the immediate agenda and enter your planned activities into your business diary. If you do this, don't forget to estimate the allocated time.

Time-management systems

You are probably already a pro at time management. After all, this is a business that requires you to keep track of other people's details in a well managed and timely manner. However, it is still easy to get overwhelmed with details and neglect your own business needs. To help keep your planning on track as well as your events and your business, there are plenty of tools to rely on and some tried-and-true systems. Walk into any office stationery store and you will find a selection of calendars, diaries, and time management systems. All are designed to help you get and stay organized.

If you are interested in dedicated software, there are some excellent project- and time-management products available that combine elements such as calendars, memo capability, and extensive list-making facilities. Day sheets and plans can be printed for your convenience.

An excellent feature of computerized time-management systems is that they don't let you forget. Once you enter an item on your to-do list, the computer automatically carries the item forward until you indicate that it is done. The software will set reminders for you in a variety of ways, depending which system you choose. See chapter 3 for more on programs that combine project management with contact or database management systems.

Social Functions, Associations, and Community Events

Your time will also be taken up by attending events in your community. To become known in your field, it is important that you get out there and meet people. Get in touch with leaders from community associations and find out whether you can attend a couple of meetings before joining. Often associations charge membership fees, which can add up if you don't reap any bankable membership benefits. You will also want a clear idea of the association's expectations of you as a member. Membership can become a very time-consuming activity, and when you are just getting your business off the ground, you cannot afford to take on extra responsibility. The local chamber of commerce is often an excellent choice to begin with. See chapter 8 for more on networking, socializing, and joining associations.

Staying Organized As You Grow

With good promotional materials and advertising, it will not take long for your business to flourish, and you will likely reach the point where you will need to hire extra help.

Even in the early stages of your new business, it is wise to have extra help organized on a casual basis. These people may be students who are available to work evenings, weekends, or during school breaks or stay-at-home moms who may not be prepared to commit to regular time or full-time jobs, but who will work occasionally when they don't have family commitments. Having this type of employee to call on is essential for the new business owner and will be a lifesaver when you are asked to produce large events. See chapter 9 for more details on employees and personnel.

One of the most difficult decisions a small-business owner must make is when to bring in help and hire employees. Do not fall into the trap of trying to save money by doing all the work yourself. The point of starting a business is to grow and prosper. If you don't hire people to help you when the business warrants it, you risk producing low-quality events, missing deadlines, and not providing good service. Do not put all the hard work you have invested in your business at risk by not knowing when it is time to grow.

As your business grows and becomes financially stable, hire a part-time or full-time assistant to take over some aspects of the business. We suggest delegating to a new employee the non-creative elements of your business, such as bookkeeping, invoicing, banking, check writing, database updating, etc. Find the balance that is right for you — and for your business.

8
Marketing, Advertising, and Promotion

The Changing Face of Advertising

The world of advertising has changed dramatically over the years and particularly in the past decade. Much of this change can be attributed to the massive growth in advertising media. Not many years ago, you could access only up to 13 channels on your TV, and television networks were as simple as A-B-C, quite literally. Now there are hundreds of stations plus cable and pay-per-view networks that offer endless viewing opportunities to the consumer.

Of course, the information age truly exploded with the internet and the advent of the World Wide Web. But even logging on to the computer and checking e-mail today is not the exercise it once was. Today, e-mail is far more cluttered with newsletters and special offers than ever before. Most of this is unsolicited e-mail advertising or "spam" — an annoying invasion of your PC often accompanied by computer viruses that can cause serious damage to your files, programs, and operating system.

Today, advertising permeates society and the competition is fierce. You see product promotion in movies and on television (not just in the commercials). Outside the home, advertisements show up on the sides of buses, but also on the roofs to get the skyscraper audience. Commuters are bombarded with massive advertising posters at airports, malls, and subway stations. Advertising is even showing up in the form of videos at the gas pump.

The latter advertising medium now has a name — outdoor. At one time, advertising was limited to print, broadcast (TV and radio), and direct mail, and outdoor simply meant billboards and signs. This is no longer the case.

Through this evolution of advertising, the whole industry began to merge into a much broader field that includes marketing and promotion and something else called branding. It can be confusing to group this convergence of services under one overarching name — and those in the industry are the first to agree. Call it what you want: communications, marketing, advertising, public relations, online marketing, interactive. For the special events business wanting to know where to begin, this chapter offers a primer.

How to Brand Your Event Planning Business

It used to be that a brand was solely a product. If you were buying Coca-Cola, and not just a cola, you were buying a brand-name product. That brand conveyed to you something of quality, an advantage that you saw was worth the extra cost or time to purchase. This concept of brand has grown to be more than just a sense of quality. It has grown to be, besides a promise of quality, something that is uniquely defined and uniquely embedded within the brand name. Today companies, even governments and political parties for that matter, are very interested in "branding" themselves.

Having a brand is considered a means of communicating one message through a unified voice to the right audience. In this cluttered world of advertising and information, no business organization can afford to send mixed messages; therefore, developing a brand is one of the most important elements of doing business today. Develop an appropriate and unique brand for your special events service and make certain that you deliver on it. Do not break your brand promise to your clients and do not try different ways to brand your services (unless you are changing roles, in which case rebranding uses an entirely different strategy).

Your branding exercise will use the strategies described below.

Developing your image

Before you embark on any advertising, marketing, or promotional activity, you need to invest some time in deciding what the overall image of your company will be. The image you project should be directly associated with the services you provide and the clients you want to serve. Are you going to plan weddings, kids' parties, or other social functions? Will you be working on sporting events or fund-raisers? Do you want to project a polished image to the corporate world? What about the high-tech industry?

Once you have decided on the overall image of your company, you can start to develop a name and logo reflecting that image.

Developing your brand promise

Along with your image, you need to define what it is about your business that will help it stand out. This is your brand promise — your point of difference. It will be a critical component of any advertising, marketing, or promotion you choose to do.

The first step is to determine the value of your service. Ask yourself the following questions:

(a) What is my service, really?

(b) What does it do?

(c) How do businesses accomplish their objectives now without my service?

(d) Why do businesses need this service? What is the value?

(e) How would I describe my potential clients (values, demographics, attitudes, actions)?

(f) How receptive is my target market likely to be to my services?

(g) If they are receptive, how often and at what times will they need my service?

(h) At what price?

(i) Is this enough information to support a credible business plan?

The next step is to define the value or attribute that makes your business different. Ask yourself these questions:

(a) Who are my competitors?

(b) In what way do they say they are best?

(c) How have they communicated this to customers?

(d) Do their promises come across as valid, compelling?

(e) Which competitors dominate which values or attributes?

(f) What attributes can my business potentially dominate?

(g) Will clients be able to understand the difference between my service and that of my competitors?

(h) Is this difference meaningful to them? In what way?

Once you have answered these questions and feel comfortable defining your point of difference, you can move on to the basic elements of creating your brand, as outlined in the rest of the chapter.

Naming your new business

Deciding what to call your new company is one of the most important decisions you will make. Quite simply, you want an uncomplicated name that provides a good idea of who your company is and what your company does. When choosing a name, consider the following questions:

(a) Is the name short, simple, and easy to spell and pronounce?

(b) Does the name clearly reflect what your company is all about?

(c) Where will your company name appear alphabetically in a telephone directory such as the Yellow Pages?

(d) Where will your name appear on an internet search engine such as Yahoo! or Google?

(e) How does the name sound over the telephone?

(f) Are there any other companies with the same name? If so, what is the nature of their business?

(g) Is the name too cute or too stuffy?

(h) Will your name be limiting to you in the future? (Think ahead. If you decide in the future to expand, you don't want to be stuck with a name that is limiting to what your business has become.)

(i) Is the name already registered to another company? See chapter 10 for a discussion of the legal aspects of choosing a business name.

(j) Is there a website available with this name?

Many business owners are inclined to use all or part of their personal name in their business name. If you are so inclined, try to combine it with a reference to the specific event services your business is offering (e.g., Kline's Conference Services).

Over the years, major brands and companies have been beaten out by competition based almost solely on the quality of their name. A potential client's very first impression of your company will most likely be based on your name, so take the time to invest some creative energy into developing a good, strong name for your business.

Designing your logo

Much like your company name, your logo should be simple, visually appealing, and in some way visually represent what your company is all about. When developing a logo, take notice of the thousands of logos we are exposed to in our everyday lives. Look for existing logos you like and ask yourself what it is you like about them. The final design is something that you might want to work on with the help of a graphic designer. When working with your graphic designer (discussed later in this chapter), ask for a few different concepts to choose from, then take those samples around to your friends and colleagues to get their opinions.

Professional Design and Production Services

Being in the special events business is no different than any other business when it comes to image. You need to take steps to ensure that all your business materials reflect your operation's professional and polished image. This section will better prepare you for the decisions you will face when developing the products used to communicate, promote, and carry out your business. Graphic design, copywriting, and photography are important services that need to be given serious consideration if you want your business to stand out from the competition.

Graphic design

Unless you have some experience in art or design, don't be tempted to create your own logo or advertising and marketing materials. Although graphic design programs are available that make designing creative pieces easier, it isn't wise to cut corners when it comes to your professional image. The success of your chosen image, name, logo, and all subsequent marketing materials lies in the hands of a professional graphic designer who can refine your thoughts and make your marketing materials appear attractive and professional to potential clients.

The costs of graphic design services can range from as little as $15 per hour to thousands per image. As a new business, you don't want to overspend, but you do want your look to be professional. Smaller firms and independent graphic designers are less expensive and will often do work at reasonable rates because they want to build up their portfolios. If you cannot afford to hire a designer, seek out friends with desktop design skills or students who need the experience. Work out a reasonable payment schedule, or perhaps offer a trade of services (this bartering or exchange of services in lieu of cash payment is also known as "contra") — perhaps plan a birthday or anniversary party in exchange.

The best way to find a good graphic designer is to get referrals from other businesses. When you start your market research, collect brochures and advertising pieces that appeal to you and find out who did the design work. Make appointments to meet with several designers to look at their portfolios and see if you can afford to hire them.

Your graphic designer is the person who will ultimately determine the overall look and feel of your entire company; he to she will design your logo, letterhead, business cards, brochure, and advertising, so it is important that the two of you get along personally. A good working relationship with a talented graphic designer can save you time and money. Remember, this is a creative field and you may have creative differences. Being comfortable with your designer will help you work through those differences without hurt feelings or the loss of time and money.

Have a clear idea of what you want before working with a designer. The more research you do prior to hiring a designer, the less his or her services will cost you in the long run. Visit your local art supply store and purchase a book of type styles, fonts, and computer graphics. Choose in advance the ones that match the look you are after. The more direction you can give the designer, the less time he or she will have to spend on your project, thus saving you money. At the same time, it is a good idea to listen to the advice of a professional. Creating a design that will project your brand is key to communicating your image instantly in a nonverbal manner.

Have the graphic artist design all of the following materials for you:

- Logo/design of company name
- Letterhead and envelopes
- Business cards
- Color brochure with photography

Hiring a professional graphic artist to design your marketing materials is one of the most important investments you can make in starting up your event planning business. Keep in mind that the cost of printing poorly designed stationery and business collateral is the same as that for printing well-designed and effective ones.

Copywriting

Once you have hired the right designer, you are ready to begin developing your marketing materials. At this point, you should consider hiring a professional copywriter to fine-tune your company's written marketing materials. The more written information you can provide the copywriter, the less time he or she will have to spend on the project, thus costing you less money. The best way to find a good copywriter is the same as for graphic designers and other professional services — by referral from other businesses.

Photography

To stand out from the crowd, consider the use of a professional photographer for your company's marketing materials. With the affordability and ease-of-use of today's digital cameras, it is tempting to try to do your own promotional photography. However, a professional photographer will make your pictures stand out and project the image you have chosen for your company.

Why You Should Advertise

As we discussed earlier, the world of advertising and marketing has changed dramatically over the years. Years ago, advertising was more a glitzy and glamorous world where gimmicks and creativity ruled. Today, advertising is a serious business that does its best when it crafts a simple message that cuts through all the competitive clutter to reach a target audience. To do this, advertising must have a foundation of sound strategy and a clear evaluation of the target market or audience before any creative element is introduced.

In a special events business, you will use advertising to —

- create brand awareness,
- show you are a leader in the industry,
- enhance your company's image,
- create a need and desire for your business,
- promote new services, and
- establish new clients.

When you are just starting out in your special events business, you do not need to invest heavily in advertising. You do, however, need to be particular about the methods you choose and the message you send. Advertising is a strategic exercise that pays dividends if done right, and the good news is that you can do much of the work yourself.

The Elements of Advertising

Developing an advertising campaign is a great opportunity to let your creativity come alive; however, there are some important core elements that should not be forgotten.

Your advertising campaign should have the following components:

- It should be easily understood.
- It should be truthful.
- It should be informative.
- It should be sincere.
- It should focus on the client.
- It should tell who, what, when, where, why, and how.

A solid campaign strategy should be built on your brand identity. Review the information on creating a brand. What do you want your customers to think of when they hear your name? Why should they choose your services over any other? How will they hear about your business? Develop a simple sentence that describes your company brand promise that sets you apart. Use this sentence as the position statement that will form the basis of all your advertising. Make sure that your position reinforces the elements listed in this section. Write down these elements and keep them handy every time you develop a new piece of advertising. They will help you stay focused and not lose sight of your client and your company brand.

Choosing Your Advertising Medium

Choosing the medium or type of advertising can be especially difficult for a small business. Television, radio, major newspapers, and magazines with large circulations are too expensive for most small businesses. Smaller community newspapers and specialized magazines can be highly effective and much more economical.

A successful advertising campaign is a long-term commitment that grows and shows a return over time. It makes better sense to put your advertising budget to use in a consistent, repetitive campaign by purchasing smaller advertisements on a regular basis than it does to put all of your dollars into a large and infrequent campaign.

Besides cost, you need to consider where your advertising will best reach its intended target. You may want to invest some time surveying prospective clients to find out where they go to find special event services. A simple phone call to survey a sample of prospects can save you a lot of money in future.

Here are some of the many options to consider when designing an advertising campaign for your event planning business.

Print

To select the publications you want to advertise in, you first need to define your goals and analyze them in terms of your budget to determine the best advertising mix to reach your target market. For example, an effective print advertising program may involve a combination of newsletters, regional magazines, trade and business publications, newspapers, and the Yellow Pages. Study your competition to find out how they are advertising, and look for alternatives to make your ads unique and more effective.

Your public library should be an excellent source to research all the publications available for you to advertise in. Make a list of the publications that interest you. Contact their sales representative and obtain a media kit. These kits will give you the advertising rates as well as the circulation and demographics of each publication. Determine the cost-effectiveness of advertising in the publication based on the circulation rates.

Cost per thousand (CPM) is the industry standard for determining the cost-effectiveness of a particular advertisement based on the publication's average circulation. For example, if a magazine is on average read by 40,000 people and the rate for a full-page ad is $800, you would divide the cost by 40. In this case, your cost would be $20 per 1,000 readers exposed to your advertisement.

If you decide to run an advertising program in a newspaper or magazine, consider running ads in a six-week series if the publication is a daily or weekly and for six months straight if it is a monthly publication.

Obviously, the timing of your ads will greatly depend on the type of clients you are trying to attract and whether there are any traditional seasons for the types of events you would like to specialize in (i.e., weddings, graduations, holidays, sports events, etc.).

Remember that running an ad does not translate into immediate new business. However, advertising also provides your existing clients with the reassurance that you are professional and that you understand the importance of keeping your name and brand in circulation.

Direct mail

Volumes have been written on the subject of direct mail advertising, and it seems to be a popular marketing tool for many companies. Direct mail can be effective for all sizes of business; however, it must be thoughtfully worded and designed to grab the attention of potential clients and create the appropriate impression and response. It should contain an offer to the recipient; in other words, there must be a call to action or a direct benefit in responding to your company's mail-out. It can be expensive to hire the services of a professional copywriter, but most will agree that without professional writing, your efforts may be for naught.

Once you have decided on the wording and design of your mail-out, you must decide whom you are going to mail it to. As a new business, you will not have a large client database and mailing list, so it may be necessary to purchase one if you want to advertise through direct mail. Many companies are in the business of selling mailing lists, and they can be found in the Yellow Pages under the headings Advertising or Direct Mail. The company you select will help you choose the right mailing list for you. As you will already have narrowed down your market, you should find it fairly straightforward to purchase an appropriate list.

If you decide to purchase a list, have the company guarantee that all the names or businesses on the list have given their permission to be contacted by other organizations. You can purchase the list on computer disk or CD-ROM. This allows you to print the addresses on your envelopes or mailing labels and merge the names with your personal letter, written on your company letterhead.

Enclose your company brochure with a personal letter and send it by first-class mail. Anything less will be perceived as junk mail and will be a waste of your time, money, and effort.

Directories

Just about every business advertises in the Yellow Pages. Advertisements vary from simple, one-line listings to half-page ads with color and graphics. Budget to place a display ad as large as you can afford and have it professionally designed. Choose the most appropriate categories to be listed under. You may want to consider advertising in more than one category.

Be sure you understand the region for the Yellow Pages, as several different regional versions of the Yellow Pages may be published in a large metropolitan area. Yellow Pages in most places are published only once a year, so don't forget to send in your ad by the deadline. Normally you will receive one free regular listing in the category of your choice, but additional listings or display ads cost extra.

Here are statistics that Yellow Pages advertises:

- 85% of adults have used the Yellow Pages at least once in the past four weeks.

- 82% contact at least one business after using the Yellow Pages.

- 66% made a purchase after referring to the Yellow Pages.

- 45% of those making a purchase had never dealt with that business before.

In addition to the Yellow Pages, there are other professional directories that have been developed by various companies targeting specific industries. These professional directories do not have as wide a distribution as a general directory such as the Yellow Pages, but they are usually more affordable and can give you some assurance that your listing is being seen by a specific targeted industry.

Sales brochure and marketing kit

When you are starting out, you will benefit from investing in a company brochure and marketing kit. This is another area where it is advantageous to retain the services of a professional graphic designer, copywriter, and photographer. When looking for a good designer and photographer, collect other companies' brochures and sales pieces that have good design and photography and contact the company's sales and marketing department to find out who did the work for them. Ask if they were happy with the price and if the work was delivered on time and on budget.

Have three different graphic design firms and photographers quote on your job. When you first meet with your chosen designer, bring samples of brochures that appeal to you. Look carefully at the designer's portfolio to determine the style of piece that you want.

Show the designer the written elements that you will be featuring in your brochure (get a word count to share with your copywriter), and let him or her know how many photographs you plan to include. If you plan on supplying your own photographs, ensure that your digital camera and software allow you to transmit high-resolution images for best-quality results. Also ask the designer for the specific computer file format he or she will require to use your photos in your brochure.

Discuss with your graphic designer the appropriate size of the brochure based on your content and what options are available to save on printing production costs (less use of color, type of paper stock, etc.).

Once the design is complete and ready to print, make sure you obtain a written price quote for final production, including a deadline for the project. Having the written quote ensures that there are no surprises that come out of additional colors, processes, etc.

Always ensure that you see a final proof and sign it off before anything is allowed to go to the printer.

If you are on a tight budget and you or a friend are creative, it is possible to design a sales piece using some of the wonderful textured and colored papers available in graphics supplies stores. There are also a number of excellent computer programs on the market that would be helpful when trying to design a sales brochure on your own. However, be realistic about your abilities and your time. Even the very talented are often better off having a professional designer work with them, if only to design a simple, one-page flyer.

You can save some money by developing your own company presentation folders. Rather than spend extra money on having a folder printed with your company logo and name, you can buy plain folders that match the paper stock of your other printed materials and use a sticker with your logo on the front. Buy the presentation folders that have the cuts already made for business cards.

You will need the services of two different types of printers: one for the materials in your sales brochure and one for your marketing kit. Establish a relationship with a smaller printer who can do one- and two-color work, such as letterhead, envelopes, business cards, gift tags, etc. You should find a printer who is close at hand and is able to turn things around quickly.

Meet with three or four printers who produce four-color work and get firm quotes in writing from all of them. The printing business is very competitive, and you will be surprised how much the prices can vary.

Printing is complicated, so make sure your price quotes include color separations. This is the process of separating color originals into the primary printing color components in negative or positive form. Also ensure that the quotes specify camera-ready art (copy that is ready for photography). Your graphic designer will need to work with your printer.

When looking at paper stock, ask to see what it looks like with both four-color printing and one- or two-color printing. Ask for sample letterhead stock to see how it works in your own computer printer.

Also ask for quotes based on running several different quantities. Sometimes the price does not vary much from one quantity to the next, and printing a greater amount is less expensive than having to run the whole order again in a few months.

Internet marketing

The internet and the World Wide Web are names that were rarely heard in business circles just a decade ago. Today, they are hard to escape, and the internet offers a number of unique opportunities for marketing your business.

First, while a newspaper advertisement may reach a local audience and a magazine advertisement may reach a national audience, the internet reaches a global audience. Better yet, it reaches an affluent global audience. Your promotional efforts on the internet reach what marketers call a "self-selected audience," meaning when someone views your website, that person has chosen to do so by using a search engine to find webpages dealing with special events.

The internet's global reach also means that someone living in another country who is organizing a meeting in your location can contract you to produce an event prior to their group's arrival.

Second, when you contract to advertise in a print publication or prepare a marketing brochure to promote your business, you commit to the content early and generally cannot make last-minute changes. For example, if you develop a print publication or prepare a marketing brochure to promote a client's event and the venue changes the day after your ad appears in print or your brochure is delivered, what do you do? Place another advertisement to show the venue change, or recall and reprint the brochure? Either way, these options are expensive. In contrast, an internet website can be changed by the hour or even by the minute, and the cost of making the change is usually no more than a few minutes of someone's time.

Finally, a website can be designed to sell your services and is capable of processing customer orders 24 hours a day, seven days a week, in effect keeping your business open around the clock.

A company website

Your company's website can be as simple or as large and complex as you want it. When you are just starting out, a few pages of information about your business, some photographs of your special events, and a link that will allow the reader to send you e-mail requests for more information will probably be a good launching pad.

If you have already paid for high-quality photographs of your events and have written promotional copy for your print brochure, you're halfway to creating your own site.

Nothing is free, and marketing your business on the internet is no exception to that rule. The good news is that the cost of internet marketing tools is continuing to fall. Setting up a simple website, such as the brochure-type site just mentioned, should not cost more than $500, and the monthly running cost (space rental from an internet service provider) is likely to be in the $20 to $30 range.

Build something fancier, and your costs will inevitably be higher. Someone is going to have to attend to the website, and this is a cost. For the simplest, brochure-type site, the cost of maintenance will be minor. Step up to a site that accepts orders or allows visitor inquiries and you will need to have someone paying constant attention to the communications generated by your site.

When you get your website up and running, how can you be sure anyone will ever visit it?

Consider creating a neutral webpage that acts as a starting point for someone interested in the special events industry, and link your website (as well as other sites that would be of interest to surfers) to this site. Many trade associations, tourist promotion boards, and similar bodies may already offer such a jumping-off point to which you can have your website added, often at no cost.

Don't forget to publicize your website on your print brochure, business card, direct mail piece, and invoices.

Beware! There are plenty of people out there selling internet snake oil. Most web designers are reputable and professional, but there some out there looking to take advantage of the not-so-tech-savvy business owner. Check with friends, neighbors, and business associates to get pointers to reliable help. Don't overlook local colleges and high schools; both may have instructor-led programs that can help you get an inexpensive website launched. In many cities, the main library now has internet resources and staff who can help you.

Start small and start cautiously. You will still be in business tomorrow even if you don't have a website with all the bells and whistles today. And almost every aspect of doing business on the internet will be less expensive tomorrow.

E-mail marketing

E-mail was one of the very first applications available on the internet. It offers companies some unique, but potentially risky, marketing opportunities.

Sending an unsolicited e-mail advertisement or "spam" is asking for trouble. Not many people like the paper junk mail they receive at home and at the office, and they tend to resent receiving unsolicited e-mail or getting "spammed."

It is possible to rent and use mailing lists for e-mail in much the same way you can for printed mail-outs. Only you can decide if the potential business this might generate is worth the almost certain backlash from frustrated recipients.

A better way of dealing with e-mail as a marketing tool is to allow people who visit your website access to more information via e-mail. For example, you could offer to send people an occasional e-mail newsletter, which will keep them updated about new services, prices, or promotions. A simple registration form on your website will allow readers to register to receive your company's news. Ensure that the form lets people know you will keep their identities and addresses private.

Using PR to Your Business Advantage

Public relations campaigns are gaining popularity as an effective marketing method. One of the key advantages to public relations is that the return on investment can be very high. Public relations in the special events business is a natural, and like word-of-mouth advertising, much will happen without you even being aware. Take control where you can by reviewing and adopting the PR tools included in this section.

Special promotions

An excellent way of promoting your business and of expanding your customer base is to organize or become involved with special events and promotions. Sometimes involvement costs little or no more than your time and a possible donation of your services. Following are a few ideas you may want to consider with for special promotions.

Open house or grand opening

Depending on the size of your facility, you may want to have a series of wine and cheese parties to promote the opening of your new business.

Small giveaways

Small gifts with your company name and phone number fall under the category of advertising specialty items. The giveaway item need not be expensive, but it should be useful and have your company name, phone number, and web address prominently printed on it. Work with a creative professional promotional-services distributor to come up with something unique and relevant to your special events business.

Fairs and trade shows

Almost every community has or public fairs and events where you can rent booth space and promote your services. These shows can be expensive, so make sure the one you plan to attend is a well-publicized event and has been successful for a number of years before committing yourself. See the Appendix for a list of fairs and trade shows specific to the special events industry.

Getting your name in the news

You can get your business profiled in the newspaper and in magazines in ways other than paying for it. You can earn it. Earned media is the method used to generate news stories about your business that get picked up by reporters and columnists. Do your homework and check out the sources that your potential clients read. The people who work at these papers and magazines need to file stories to their editors on a daily, weekly, or semiweekly basis. Radio reporters often have several deadlines in a day! If you want to get their notice, there are different ways to go about it. Here are some pointers to earn you media attention:

(a) At your next public event (or an event where you have sought permission to invite the press), send out a press release in advance. See Sample 5 for an example of a press release. Make sure you send it directly to the reporter or desk you want to target (e.g., business section, lifestyle), then follow up the day of the event, if possible. Make the event sound intriguing and worth going to.

(b) Have a media kit at the event. This should include your company brochure, a press release on the event, and any relevant background material. Enclose your business card.

(c) Issue a media advisory with enough detail about your event or services to catch the interest of newspaper or magazine editors. See Sample 6 for an example of a media advisory. Offer an interview. Make sure you are aware of the publishing deadlines; call to find out what they are.

(d) Call up magazines and newspapers to find out their editorial plans in advance, then submit ideas and stories that fit in with their special inserts or themes. Often this approach will require some commitment to paid advertising, but it can be an extremely effective way to generate more space and reach a targeted audience.

Socializing for success

One of the advantages of a special events business is that almost everyone you know and meet could be a potential customer. Even in casual social situations, the conversations usually come around to what people do for a living, and without being too obvious, you can make new clients just about anywhere.

When someone expresses interest in your company, give them a business card (you should have a supply of business cards with you at all times) and offer to send a company brochure or invite them to visit your office. A satisfied client can pass your name along to several people, who in turn can pass your name on to more people, and so on.

Word-of-mouth advertising is the most cost-effective way to promote your business. Most owners of successful special events companies are very active and social people involved with many organizations in their community. It is feasible to make new business contacts and find potential clients at any place you might frequent, such as —

- your place of worship,
- school parent association meetings,
- political meetings,
- health club or country club,
- hair salon,

PRESS RELEASE

<u>For immediate release</u>

HEADLINE IS ALL CAPS, HAS AN ACTIVE VERB, AND IS ON ONE LINE
(Example: Jade Palace Hosts Global Launch of Wonder Widgets)

LOCATION — Open with an angle — hook your audience. Briefly outline WHO, WHAT, WHERE, WHEN, AND HOW.

The press needs a good story, but they receive many releases in a single day. Make yours stand out by getting the story out at the beginning. This is the "inverted pyramid" style of writing. Get the most important information out in your first and second paragraphs.

By the third paragraph, you should have a quote from a key person involved in your event (e.g., company president, spokesperson, VIP). Again, keep it short and make sure it adds interest or insight to your story. A quote should sound natural — as it would if spoken.

"This product is revolutionizing the way widgets work," said Bob Black, CEO of World-Wide Widgets. "Every business that deals in widgets should attend the launch. Once you see the new widget in action, you will know there is no turning back."

By the fourth paragraph you will want to get into more detail. This could be a bulleted list outlining the event agenda or more details on how the event came to be.

The fifth paragraph should be another quote, or quotes, to support, but not repeat, the information contained in the first quote and in the story overall.

Any technical points should be included in the last paragraph. Read over your release to be sure that it answers who, what, where, when, and how. If you need to add information, use a "backgrounder," as news editors prefer simple, one-page releases.

-30-

#

(Use either mark to indicate the end of the release.)

Supply information before the contact name, such as any website that will provide further information, or indicate that a backgrounder is attached with more information on the event.

Contact: name, title, phone number. (Ensure the contact is available when the release goes out!)

TIPS: Target your news release to the most relevant news and customer sources (10 to 20 targets). Where applicable, get permission to have the press interview or photograph a VIP. Develop several story lines with a human-interest angle. Call your targeted sources after faxing the release and offer your stories and interview/photography availability. Be aware of press times! Weekly community papers have early deadlines — find out ahead of time by calling the news sources. That way, you can get your event in before press deadlines.

MEDIA ADVISORY

Today's date

To: Name
Title (should be the editor)
Name of the Paper

MEDIA ADVISORY HEADLINE: THE "WHAT" KEPT SHORT, ALL CAPS

(Essentially, the media advisory gives brief and intriguing details on your event. Make sure that it includes the what, who, when, where, and contact and you will be fine.)

WHAT: Capture the media's attention by inserting the location of the event. Briefly describe the event. Offer enough details to make it worth attending, but not so many that the media can skip it altogether. The advisory should entice the media to attend!

WHO: Give the names of the people organizing the event and any VIPs involved. Describe the attendees (e.g., 350 members of such and such organization). If interviews are available, provide contact information.

WHEN: Date and time. Indicate the time for cameras and audio before the main event or arrival of speakers, VIPs.

WHERE: Help the media get to the event. Detail any information or offer a map if it is an unusual location or if parking will be difficult. If press credentials are needed, make it known.

(Fax the media advisory to your target media at least 24 hours before the event. More time will be necessary if significant travel or media registration is required — sometimes necessary at major events or where security is high. Follow up the day of with a phone call, if possible. NEVER MAKE A MEDIA ADVISORY MORE THAN ONE PAGE! AND DON'T TURN IT INTO A PRESS RELEASE.)

-30-

Contact: Name, title, company, phone number, and contact information for the day of the event. This is a key piece of information. Don't ever leave it out!

- community center,
- card club,
- alumni association, or
- any other place where you meet people on a regular basis.

Almost everyone you meet is a potential client, so make sure your friends and acquaintances are aware of what you do for a living.

Networking, networking, networking

Networking is the exchange of information or services among individuals, groups, or institutions. Networking can be as simple as having lunch with a friend who is well connected in the business community who may give you names of a few potential clients to contact, to attending a more formal, organized networking group.

There are a number of these networking organizations active in North America, to which many large companies and corporations belong. Corporations can generate your most profitable events. Most businesses hold events on a regular basis, not just during the holiday season. Many companies recognize employee anniversaries, birthdays, promotions, and retirements. They may also organize employee picnics and holiday parties. Most businesses do not have the time or personnel to devote to organizing these events. Forming a good relationship with a special events company can solve many of their dilemmas.

Association memberships

Numerous organizations exist in every community that you should consider joining and becoming actively involved with. Always ask to attend one or two meetings before committing to any membership. Ask about benefits and expectations — in writing, preferably. Do not jump into anything without due diligence. Taking a membership in a business organization costs money and involves time, so find those that provide the best networking opportunities and generate the most business. Certainly, information-sharing is an important element of collaboration with colleagues and leaders in your field, but it is their potential for offering referrals to clients and projects that really pays off — and is vital in the beginning. See the Appendix for a list of industry associations throughout North America. Following is a list with more detailed information on a few organizations you might want to consider as well as an estimate of what your annual dues might be.

Tourism, convention, or visitors' bureau

If you live in a community that is a tourist destination or has hotel and meeting facilities for conventions, a membership in this type of organization could be very important to your business. Attending the meetings and functions will give you an opportunity to meet people involved with the tourism and hospitality industry.

Most tourism organizations also publish a confidential list of upcoming conventions that includes a contact name with an address and telephone number. If you make a point of getting to know the people within the tourism organization, they can be a good source of leads. They are also usually very loyal to members who have a proven track record of providing good service. Annual dues are $200 to $400.

Board of trade or chamber of commerce

Most members of this type of organization are industry leaders and business owners in a community. Meetings are usually held at breakfast or lunch and feature a guest speaker. In one large city, the board of trade offers a once-a-month function called Business after Business. This function takes place in a different hotel ballroom or other large venue every month, and members can book a table to display their services for a fee.

The general public is invited to attend this function, which gives the companies involved a chance to meet face-to-face with potential clients for two hours. Most members will confirm that they take away more than enough business to justify the time and expense involved. When you consider that the attendees are busy people, they hold very good potential for someone looking to establish a special events business — especially for meetings and conferences. Annual dues are $300 to $600.

Meeting professionals international

Meeting Professionals International (MPI) is an international organization of meeting planners and affiliated suppliers; most chapters are in the United States and Canada. Local chapters have monthly meetings, and a membership in this type of organization offers excellent potential for education and referrals, especially from suppliers that you get to know. Annual dues at time of printing are $350.

Special events societies

The International Special Events Society (ISES) and the Canadian Special Events Society (CSES) attract members in the event industry, such as special event planners, caterers, decorating companies, tent rental companies, entertainment companies, and party equipment rental companies. Membership offers excellent opportunities for getting leads on upcoming special events and meetings and for learning who to contact. Annual dues for ISES are $350 US; annual dues for CSES are $200 CDN.

Belonging to an organization is a commitment of your time as well as money, so be prepared to attend the meetings and volunteer for functions if you want your membership to pay for itself in future business. Most organizations and associations are listed in the Yellow Pages, and notices of meetings are usually listed once a week in the business section of the newspaper. One of the other advantages of taking a membership in a large organization is that they will then provide you with a complete membership roster, which will help in starting your potential client database and mailing list.

Measuring Advertising Effectiveness

Get into the habit of asking new clients how they heard about your company, and after a few months you should have a good feel for what type of advertising and marketing is working for you. Remember, it can take up to six months for an advertising and marketing program to show any visible return, so don't expect miracles overnight.

It is a good idea to create an expense breakdown of your advertising and marketing and compare the costs with your project and event revenues. Sample 7 shows an example of such a breakdown for both a studio/office and a home-based business.

ADVERTISING AND PROMOTIONS EXPENSE BREAKDOWN

* Studio/office:	Monthly	Quarterly	Annually
Yellow Pages (2" x 2" ad)	$150	$450	$1,800
Opening promo and yearly			1,250
Print advertising (10x)	250	750	3,000
Direct mail (4x)		1,000	4,000
TOTAL	$400	$2,200	$10,050

*Note: Budget is based on spending from 3% to 5% of gross projected sales ($250,000) on advertising.

*Home-based:	Monthly	Quarterly	Annually
Yellow Pages (¾ ad)		$48	$570
Opening promo and yearly			540
Print advertising (December)			250
Direct mail (2x)			1,890
TOTAL		$48	$3,250

*Note: Budget is based on spending from 3% to 5% of gross projected sales ($65,000) on advertising.

9
Employees and Personnel

Being a Sole Owner/Operator

In the start-up phase and early stages of your new business, it is unlikely that you will be in a financial position to hire employees or contract workers. For that reason, be prepared to work some long hours. Of course, you likely knew that was part of the package when you work in the events industry. As in most new ventures, the sole owner of a special events company must wear many hats and be responsible for all aspects of the business. The following list is just a snapshot of the duties you will need to attend to:

(a) Seeking business opportunities

(b) Creating proposals

(c) Planning events

  (i)   Developing the event concept

  (ii) Creating the event budget

  (iii) Working with suppliers

  (iv) Managing the event

(d) Purchasing equipment and supplies

(e) Processing business by phone or fax and sending out quotations

(f) Managing schedules and time lines

(g) Managing the office

(h) Managing advertising and promotions

(i) Accounting/bookkeeping, receivable and payable

(j) Banking

(k) Filing and keeping all records and materials organized

Your personal life will dictate to some extent the best way to organize your time, but if you get into the habit of scheduling your events and time lines and stick with it, you will be surprised how much can be accomplished by one person in a regular workweek. Consider the following scheduling advice as you plan events:

- Always expect the unforeseen. (What appears small can always turn into something bigger.)

- Establish a realistic event time line for each event from the start. Often it is said, "Start at the beginning," and this is helpful. Every detail must be charted out. Through this process, you will discover if it is possible to produce the event entirely by yourself, or if you will need to hire a part-time worker or contract out part of your event.

- Depending on the size of the event, you might have to create several time lines (e.g., for advertising and marketing, registration or RSVPS, production and delivery for materials and supplies, or pre-event programs, if any — as in receptions or wine-and-cheese gatherings that occur prior to a gala event). Some events require a minute-by-minute itinerary, especially those that have speeches by VIPS and media attendance.

- Name these specific time lines and incorporate them into a large rollout on the overall event time line.

- Be sure to confirm with your suppliers their time lines and areas of responsibility.

- Make sure your suppliers also know your time lines well and that they confirm that your suggested time lines are realistic.

With success, there will come a day when you realize that you will not be able to produce an event or several events entirely on your own. This is okay! This is good! Indeed, you may come to the conclusion that it is more profitable to contract help on a casual, part-time, or regular basis to cover off certain aspects of your events or business.

Think about this and be sensible. If you are not a bookkeeper, there is no sense wasting your time and effort taking care of your books. Instead, hire a bookkeeper so that you can spend your time seeking new business opportunities or working on events that generate more money than you saved by doing the books yourself.

Casual Labor and Seasonal Helpers

Even if you decide to run your business alone, there will be times when the volume and size of your events makes it physically impossible to operate effectively by yourself. You may realize that you don't have time to write that press release or process the data on conference registrants, and perhaps you will find yourself overwhelmed and will welcome help. You may also hire because you realize that your event could be improved by hiring someone with expertise in a certain field. For example, you might consider hiring a seasoned professional to provide the floral arrangements and décor at a large gala. Or you might consider hiring a media relations expert and security personnel if you are holding a major event with celebrities. Here is some information on where to find casual helpers as well as some of the legal considerations of hiring.

Where to look for extra hands

University students are a good resource for casual help during the year. Contact the student employment office of your local college or university in the late fall to post your notice of employment wanted.

As well, many full-time homemakers who are not interested in regular employment are willing to work on call or on a part-time basis. Find this type of help by telling friends or acquaintances that you are looking to hire someone. Remember to spread the word by posting a notice in your gym, place of worship, or social club.

As the owner of an event company, you will soon find that you have individuals coming to you seeking employment opportunities in the special events field. It is not uncommon to have many individuals offering their time on a volunteer basis to gain experience in the industry.

Know your legal responsibilities

All personnel policies operate within a legal framework. Among the many governmental regulations for employers today are the minimum wage laws, fair employment regulations, requirements for withholding income taxes and other items from employees' paychecks for the federal, provincial, or state government, and public policies regarding safety in the workplace and equal opportunity. Before you begin hiring, check the current regulations with your local government employment department.

The laws vary by state, province, or country as to the maximum amount a person can earn as a casual laborer before the employer must register him or her as an employee and deduct taxes. The minimum wage laws also vary, and you should find out what the legal requirements are in your area before hiring. In some areas, training wages can apply for students or for those just entering the workforce. Depending on the duties performed, a part-time worker or contractor will make anywhere from minimum wage upward. You may also want to pay someone on a project basis. One advantage to paying a flat project fee is you know right from the outset what your worker costs will be. However, as with all aspects of your business, take your time to decide on the type of help you need. Ask other companies that hire for similar positions if they'd be willing to recommend workers to you, and ask them about the going rate.

Put details in writing

We recommend you always write a job description that outlines the job responsibilities and skills that are required. That way you understand better what your needs are and you have a written policy that outlines what is expected from the person you hire. Not having a clear job description can be very frustrating to an employee, for it is difficult to foresee all the different duties of the job. And the lack of a clear job description can lead to some differences of opinion between an employer and an employee, which is less than productive for any special events business. See Sample 8 for an example of a job description.

If you require your employee/contractor to drive on behalf of your company, it is your responsibility to compensate employees for gas and mileage, over and above their hourly pay. Be sure to discuss all wages and extraordinary expenses with the worker before hiring. We recommend that you put your agreement in writing, and that

SAMPLE 8
JOB DESCRIPTION

Position Information:

Position Title: Events Manager

Position Level: Senior

Company: XYZ Events

Location: Vancouver, BC

POSITION DESCRIPTION:

XYZ Events is known for delivering outstanding, innovative, and award-winning events in the Pacific Northwest. We are seeking a high-energy, results-oriented, creative person with a proven track record to fill the position of Events Manager. The successful candidate will oversee the development and budgets of several of the events and conferences our company produces, reporting directly to the President, XYZ Events.

DUTIES AND RESPONSIBILITIES:

1. Participates in the planning and establishment of goals and objectives for both events and conferences, with respect to budgets, speakers, facilities, technology, equipment, logistical requirements, and other related issues.

2. Evaluates program/event histories, budget considerations, contractual provisions, and planning committee recommendations and provides input for future events and projects.

3. Serves as principal liaison between contractors, organizers, faculty, and administrators with respect to all facets of the logistical operations and support of multiple programs and events.

4. Will oversee the marketing and design team with respect to marketing materials, to include brochures and flyers, for events and conferences.

5. Responsible for budget planning as well as administering the purchasing of supplies and/or equipment for specific events and conferences.

6. Will assist in or contribute to the planning, coordination, development, and implementation of new business development.

MINIMUM JOB REQUIREMENTS:

High school diploma or equivalent with at least five years' experience directly related to the event responsibilities listed above.

KNOWLEDGE, SKILLS, AND ABILITIES REQUIRED:

- Strong interpersonal and communication skills.
- A thorough understanding of financial reports, accounting, budgeting, and cost control procedures.
- An excellent working knowledge of technology and equipment.
- Ability to create and edit written materials.
- Strong negotiating and management skills.
- Solid experience in the development and implementation of short- and long-range goals.
- A thorough knowledge of meeting and event planning principles, requirements, and procedures.

INSTRUCTIONS TO APPLY:

Please send resume and salary requirements to:

XYZ Events

both you and the employee/contractor sign the agreement, so that you both have a copy of your arrangements should problems arise regarding specific responsibilities in future.

Talk to your part-timer/volunteer or contractor about possible full-time work that may become available. If you are lucky enough to find someone with creative and artistic abilities and your special events business is growing, you might want to train that person to be your assistant. The events you produce are a reflection of your company, so it is important that you oversee and train an employee who takes on this responsibility to ensure high standards of quality are maintained.

Hiring an Assistant

As your business grows and prospers, you will want to hire either a full-time or part-time assistant. Even if he or she appears to easily fulfill your job description, choose this person carefully, as you will spend a lot of time together and he or she will represent your company. This person must be compatible with you and be capable of running your business when you are away.

Hire someone who is personable, self-motivated, organized, a quick learner, and a team player. These traits are more important than any previous special event production experience. If the person has the above attributes, you can teach him or her anything he or she does not already know. This person can be trained to take on management duties, which will free up some of your time and allow you to concentrate on selling and marketing your services. Hire someone who is creative and able to get along well with your suppliers and your customers.

Again, the pay will be dictated by the type of work to be performed. Check with other companies that hire for similar positions to get the going rate. If the person you wish to hire has experience, expect to pay more. At times, you will find that the person you wish to hire has a fee in mind and will not settle for less. Some people are worth paying that extra for, as they can often deliver much more to your bottom line.

Hiring an Office Manager/Bookkeeper

Depending on the size of your business and the sales revenue, the position of office manager/bookkeeper can be either part-time or full-time. When you reach the point of needing this type of employee, it is probably wise to first bring someone in on a part-time basis and increase the hours as the business warrants. Maintaining accurate books and records is essential to your business, and as your company becomes more successful and the events become more complex, these tasks will take more time.

Office managers/bookkeepers are usually in charge of some or all of the following business functions:

- Accounts payable and receivable
- Payroll
- Banking
- Regular filing of local and federal taxes
- Tracking of employee expense accounts
- Updating the customer and supplier database
- Maintaining company insurance, business licenses, and corporate records

- Creating monthly financial statements
- Purchasing office supplies and stationery
- Office equipment supplies and maintenance
- Postage and mailing
- Tax preparation

By no means should this be considered an exhaustive list. Remember to create a job description before hiring (see Sample 8). If you are unsure about a job description, visit job boards for reference purposes. Sources include the internet, newspapers, libraries, and job banks.

Your office manager/bookkeeper should be familiar with all aspects of the business and be able to comfortably answer phone calls and deal with customers if necessary. If you only need help of this nature on a part-time basis, one or two days a week, it may be possible to hire someone who does this type of work for several different companies. In this case, it would be preferable for that person to work on contract and bill you for services once or twice a month. Don't think you have to put someone on your payroll. As always, check around, as fees will vary depending on experience brought to the job and the responsibilities the job entails.

Hiring and Keeping Good Employees

Finding and hiring the right employees for your business is not an easy task. Keeping good employees after you have hired and trained them is an even more difficult task, but one that is essential to the continued growth and success of your company. One of the most difficult decisions a small-business owner will make is determining the right time to hire personnel.

Many small-business owners are reluctant to hire personnel for fear of bringing someone into their business who is dishonest or is just itching to leave to work with or become the competition. If you let these fears hold you back from hiring employees, they will also prevent you from attaining growth and increased profitability.

Many small businesses fail or never move to higher income and profit levels because the owner is not willing to expand the business by hiring employees. Do not waste all the time, effort, and money that you have spent in starting your business by not knowing when it is time to expand and hire. For a special events business to be successful, there must be someone to handle the creative side of the company as well as the business side. When the volume of business reaches a level that you, as sole owner, are unable to handle, it is time to hire or the whole business will stagnate.

Again, make sure you take the time to properly prepare a job description. There is nothing more frustrating then hiring someone and then realizing that he or she does not have the skills and/or experience to match the job or project. Usually, bad employees or contractors are the result of an employer not doing his or her homework. Know what you expect of an employee before you start looking.

Before hiring anyone, you should do the following:

(a) Create a job description, which includes —

Job title

Responsibilities

Duties

Expected hours and work days

Vacation policy (when vacations can and cannot be taken)

Paid holidays

Remuneration

(b) Outline required knowledge and qualifications:

Education level

Previous experience (in years)

Special skills (computer and keyboard skills, customer service, etc.)

Special requirements (CGA, driver's license, etc.)

By detailing your own needs before you hire, you are much more likely to find an employee who will meet those needs.

Commonsense guidelines to hiring employees

Keeping yourself and your workplace healthy and productive is easier if you have the right people working for you. While there are no guaranteed methods for hiring, there are some commonsense practices you can apply.

Do not hire friends or relatives

Hiring friends or relatives as employees rarely works out. It is often difficult for friends or relatives to be treated as employees and to treat you as an employer. If a friend or relative does not work out and you must let him or her go, you not only lose an employee, but you risk losing a personal relationship.

Ask for recommendations

Ask business associates, whose judgment you respect, if they can recommend potential employees. Personal references can often provide the most suitable people.

Contact job placement departments

Recruit potential employees by using the job placement departments at schools, colleges, and universities. Today, most colleges offer special event training programs, so you may want to start with them first. If you are seeking someone to handle new business development, you might want to post notices in the marketing departments of universities and colleges.

Check with your local chapter of Meeting Planners International (MPI), the International Special Events Society (ISES), and the Canadian Special Events Society (CSES) to see if they have job boards. See the Appendix for a complete list of industry associations.

Advertise for help

Advertising in newspaper or trade publications can be effective, but it can also be expensive and generate many more resumes than you have time to process. When writing a classified ad, be very specific about what your requirements are, the educational and work background you are looking for, and what the hours and remuneration will be.

Use job application forms

Purchase job application forms from your local stationery store and have each potential job applicant fill one out. Make sure you have a complete job history, educational background, and references from each applicant. Make a short list of the most qualified people and arrange personal interviews.

Check references

If you are serious about hiring someone after an interview, make sure you check his or her references to verify employment history. Tell the reference what the duties and tasks are and ask if the person you are calling about is qualified to take on this role.

Commonsense guidelines to keeping good employees

Just as there are some commonsense practices to follow in hiring good employees, there are some simple, yet effective methods for keeping them. It is surprising how far these tips can take you towards being a positive and guiding influence on your employees.

Communication

Have an open-door policy with all your employees. Build an atmosphere in which your employees feel free to speak up and know they will be listened to. Schedule an hour each week to sit down with your staff over a cup of coffee to get any grievances or problems out in the open. This is also a great time to have brainstorming sessions and come up with creative ways to market your products and services. Make your employees feel that they are really part of the team and important to the success of your business.

Consistency

Set standards and insist that they be met. If you can force yourself to be consistent, you will make it easy for employees to work for you, even if your standards are high. Have your standards in writing in the form of a personnel manual. Make sure that all new employees read and understand this manual at the time they are hired. If employees know what to expect, you will eliminate any future misunderstandings. If you want to curb, for example, personal phone calls, surfing the internet, absenteeism, smoking on the work site, improper dress, gum chewing, etc., make your rules known during the hiring process. Your employees will give you what your actions say you want.

Recognition

Your employees must have pride in what they do if their work is to be good. Make it known at all times to each employee that he or she is part of your team and a huge contributor to your success. Don't forget this, for you truly are only as good as your team. Praise your staff for a job well done and let them know when you receive written or verbal praise about them or your company from a client.

Compensation

Pay your employees fairly and according to what the job market in your area requires. Give them increases once they have proven themselves. One well-paid, well-trained, motivated, capable employee will serve your needs much better than three underpaid, mediocre, indifferent ones. Hiring and rehiring is an expensive and time-consuming process, which can lead to lost productivity and projects.

Evaluation

Evaluate your employees. An evaluation allows you to assess the employee's performance, plan the training and development they may still require, exchange opinions, and generally build a better working relationship. Employees like to know where they stand and to have an opportunity to improve through constructive criticism and evaluation, rather than wait until there is a complaint.

Commissions and share options

If you have an employee who is hired to promote the company and bring in new business, it may make sense to work out a commission structure on top of a base salary or hourly wage. This type of pay structure usually motivates the employee to work hard and deliver more results.

Most commission structures are based on attaining set sales goals, and it is therefore more appropriate for a company that has been in business for a few years to use this type of structure. A share option plan is an agreement between you and your employees in which you give your employees the right to purchase shares in your company for a certain price. The option is held open for a certain length of time. Such plans provide financial inducements for your employees to become shareholders. Granting share options can be complicated from a legal point of view, and you will need to deal with your lawyer if you are going to consider this offering.

A successful business owner will realize that fringe benefits, health and hospital insurance, paid vacations, profit-sharing, fair wages, good working conditions, and concern for employees are all part of building a happy, dedicated, productive staff. Keeping your employees happy will help advance your business and will create an image of your special events company as an excellent place to work. Your employees are part of your good public relations, for they will promote your business by word-of-mouth through all their social and business connections.

10
Making the Business Legal

Your Legal Structure

Before you complete many of the other legal requirements mentioned later in this chapter, you will first need to decide in what legal form you will carry on your business. Your choices of the form of legal entity include a sole proprietorship, a partnership, a limited partnership, and an incorporated company. There are tax advantages and disadvantages to each of the possible business structures, and incorporation is governed by state or provincial laws. You should obtain legal and tax advice before making your final decision.

Sole proprietorship

As the name indicates, a sole proprietorship is a business structure in which there is only one owner. This is the simplest way to carry on business and may have tax advantages for you early in the operation of the business, for any losses you incur may be deducted from income you may make from other sources.

Just because you are the sole owner doesn't mean to say that you could not have one or more employees, but the profits and losses from the business are all yours.

Partnership

If you have two or more people who will be owners of the business, then you can create a partnership (if you decide not to incorporate a company, as discussed later in this chapter). Partnerships can be quite complicated from a legal point of view, as many of the terms of a partnership agreement must be created by your lawyer. Partnerships have the advantage that losses may also be deducted from your other income. Their large disadvantage is that each partner is personally liable for any losses or breach of contract, even if the other partners do not pay their fair share.

If you form a partnership, you should consider how you will buy out the interest of your partner or partners if they become disabled or die. You may wish to consider obtaining life insurance on each partner, which is payable to the partnership or to the remaining partners. As well, take all precautions if you realize the partnership is not a good fit personality-wise. If your misgivings are strong, it is perhaps better that you simply forgo the partnership altogether.

Limited partnerships

A limited partnership involves a silent partner who may contribute money to your business and receive a share of the profits, but who would not be actively involved in running the business. Limited partnerships must be set up in a special fashion, and it is unlikely that you would be able to create one without the assistance of a lawyer.

Incorporation

Whether you are a one-person business or there are two or more of you in business together, you can incorporate a company in which to conduct your business. To avoid confusion, you should note that the word "company" is often used to describe a sole proprietorship or some other type of business, and the proper legal word is "corporation," not company.

All states and provinces allow one or more persons to incorporate a business, but there are significant fees for the privilege of creating a corporation and usually subsequent annual fees to keep your corporation in good standing.

Having a corporation is the most sophisticated way of carrying on a business, and customers will be more impressed than if you were a sole proprietorship or partnership. Corporations offer great flexibility, for you may issue shares in your corporation to your co-owners, in differing proportions and with different rights for those shares. For example, if a relative were prepared to invest in your business but you did not want him or her to have any say in the day-to-day operations, you could create a special class of nonvoting shares for that person.

There are various tax implications — both advantages and disadvantages — to having a corporation. Some states and provinces have lower tax rates for small corporations, and you can have the profits of your special events business taxed at a lower rate, as long as you do not pay out all of the profits to the shareholders of your corporation by way of salaries or dividends.

Corporations generally have the advantage of limited liability, which means that the individual shareholders would not be personally liable for debts of the corporation if the business went under. You should note that this protection of limited liability does not extend to negligence (e.g., if you or your co-owners cause some personal damage to someone during the course of the business, then you or your co-owners, and possibly your company, could all be sued for negligence). The limited liability of a corporation extends only to its debts.

Unfortunately, sophisticated lenders or grantors of credit, such as banks and major suppliers, often want the individual shareholders to guarantee the corporation's debts, thereby taking away the advantage of limited liability.

Although it is certainly possible to incorporate a business yourself, you should consider using the services of a lawyer. (When your company grows and your events become more complex, it is also wise to have a lawyer who can review or help create business contracts. See chapter 6 for more on contracts.) The paperwork for incorporation itself is not usually very difficult, but the advice that the lawyer can provide both before and after incorporation can be invaluable. If you do decide to incorporate, you must rigorously carry out all of the requirements set out, including what to do after incorporation and what to do each year to keep your corporation in good standing (i.e., not being canceled by the state or province because of your failure to file any required annual documents).

Remember that there will be continuing costs relating to maintaining your corporation, including annual filing fees, as noted above, but also the additional cost of preparing a separate income tax return for your corporation.

As with partnerships, if there is to be more than one owner in the corporation, you should consider obtaining life and disability insurance on the other shareholders so that a shareholder can be bought out with the insurance if he or she dies or becomes disabled.

Leave It to the Professionals

No one starting a new business wants to spend more money than he or she has to, but the time will come when your new business needs professional advice on matters of law or accounting.

Accounting and law are highly specialized areas, and each is subject to constant change. It is difficult for the small-business owner to keep up with these changes and still run a profitable business.

Although professional advice is expensive, it is often necessary to avoid costly mistakes. If you are unsure of legalities that affect your business or you are confused about proper accounting procedures, you should use the services of a qualified accountant and lawyer.

For example, before deciding on whether to incorporate, seek the advice of a professional tax accountant who can advise you on whether it is best for you to incorporate at the beginning, or whether it is better to delay that decision until the size of the business increases. After you have talked to the tax accountant, consult a lawyer if you need one.

Any lawyer or professional you engage must have good communication skills. A good lawyer should make it easy for you to ask questions and should explain things in simple terms. Of course, the fee structure is the other important consideration when hiring a lawyer or other professional. You should never hesitate to ask about the fee at the outset, and you should ask for frequent billings so that you can always keep an eye on how your legal costs are rising.

It is wise to plan for your professional services early in your business cycle to take the time to select who you want to act for your new business and to check credentials. The other option is to wait until you have a problem. This method can be perilous. If your mind is occupied with a problem, it is not always clear enough to choose an adviser wisely. If the problem is serious and you are under stress, you may even engage the wrong person entirely and spend more time and money than you need to. It is better to establish a comfortable working relationship from the beginning. You do not need to pay a king's ransom for professional services if you prepare yourself and your business properly.

Choosing Your Name — Legally

Choosing the right name for your business is important. Chapter 8 discusses some issues to consider when choosing your name to make it suitable for your business and to help customers remember it. But there are legal considerations as well.

First, file and protect the name you have chosen. You can always operate your business under your proper name (e.g., Melanie's Special Events), but if you choose a fictitious name (e.g., Events for Every Occasion), or your name implies that more than one person owns the business (e.g., Melanie and Company), most jurisdictions require that such names be registered. This is done by filing a "fictitious name statement" with county or provincial authorities.

When you register a fictitious name, it will be checked against previously filed names to ensure the name has not been taken by another business. This is for your protection too.

Many people start their businesses and do not register the name. This can be a costly mistake. You may operate for a few months or longer, all the while spending time and money to get your company name recognized and respected, then one day you receive a registered letter telling you to stop using it. Too late, you find out that the name is already used and protected by someone else. You may even be liable for damages. Once your name is on file, it cannot be used by anyone else.

It is a good idea to have two, or even three, names ready before you register. That way, if your first choice is rejected, you will have another name ready and you won't have to start all over again. A quick (though not foolproof) way to check the availability of the name is to scan your local telephone book.

In Canada, you can have a name search done through the provincial ministry that handles incorporations. This will also tell you if the name is registered out of province. This process takes about a week, and there is a small fee, generally under $50.

In the United States, your city or county clerk will tell you if the name is available for use.

In some states and provinces, it is also possible to have a "trading name" for your corporation, which gives you the flexibility to change the name in the future, should the nature of your business change or become more comprehensive. If you incorporate under the name Melanie's Special Events Inc., for example, you may later find the name to be a disadvantage when you have branched out into other services.

When choosing your trading name or your actual incorporated name, you should also keep in mind the advantage of having a name, which is self-advertising. Although there are disadvantages to having a name like Melanie's Special Events Inc., which you may later want to change, in the beginning it at least tells your customers exactly what your business is. A name like Melanie's Enterprises Inc. does not describe your business, so the listing of your name in the white pages, or in any other listing where your name only is displayed, generates no publicity for you.

You will probably need to consult a lawyer if you wish to have a trading name.

Insurance Requirements

Always discuss your insurance needs with a professional. Be sure to let your insurance company know that you produce events.

If you are starting your business out of your home, you will find that your standard homeowner policy is not enough to meet the needs of your business. It will not cover things such as lawsuits, damages, or accidents that may result from your business.

If you are starting your business in leased or rental space, you will also have to consider business liability insurance. An insurance professional can help set up a policy that is right for you.

Some types of insurance you may want to consider are as follows:

(a) *General liability:* Covers incidents that happen within or outside your premises, such as an employee being involved in an accident, a person falling over in your office, etc.

(b) *Special event liability:* Covers activities and events of all types conducted at halls, arenas, community centers, theaters, stadiums, and similar publicly or privately owned facilities.

(c) *Product liability:* Protects against a lawsuit by a customer or client who used your product or service and, as a result, sustained bodily injury or property damage from it.

(d) *Automobile liability:* Covers other people's property, other automobiles, persons in other vehicles, and persons in the insured automobile. If you are using your car for business purposes, exclusively or occasionally, it is important that you have your premium cover business use. It is possible that your current motor vehicle insurance policy has just a premium based on personal use. Problems could occur if there were an accident and it was discovered that your car was used for business purposes.

(e) *Fire and theft liability:* Covers against damage and loss due to fire or theft.

(f) *Business interruption insurance:* The indirect loss from a fire or theft can be greater than the loss itself. You will not only have the cost of carrying on the business temporarily from some other location, you will also possibly have losses because you will have lost your accounts receivables records or other records that are essential to your business.

(g) *Personal disability insurance:* Covers the possibility of your being disabled for a short or long period of time. This insurance pays you a certain monthly amount if you are permanently disabled, or a portion of that amount if you are partially disabled, but capable of generating some income.

There may be other forms of insurance you should have, and your insurance broker is the best person to discuss these with.

Leases and Rental Agreements

Apart from setting up the form of legal entity you will use, the most important legal matter to be considered is the form of any lease you might wish to enter into. If you lease space on a month-to-month basis, the terms of the written or verbal lease agreement will be much less important, because if you are unhappy with anything the landlord does, you can always give notice and find premises elsewhere. The big disadvantage is, of course, that a landlord can also give you notice, and you could find your business out on the street.

A written, long-term lease has the advantage of giving you security of your whereabouts for a fixed time, but also obliges you to keep paying for that lease, whether or not your business is successful.

While it is up to you to consider the practicalities of any location you propose to lease (see chapter 2 for a discussion of location considerations), you should probably hire a lawyer to review any proposed lease. Leases can be tedious to read, but you should not just rely on your lawyer reading it. At a very minimum, you will need to know the answers to the following questions when you and your lawyer review the proposed lease:

(a) Is it clear how much the rent is? Many leases have a fixed basic rent, but on top of that rent, you are also required to pay a proportionate share of the operating costs for the building that contains your proposed premises. These operating costs, which include the property taxes, insurance, utilities, cleaning, and other costs incurred by the landlord in running that particular building, can be as much as the basic rent itself. Most landlords will be vague about the operating costs of the building (in part because they have to estimate the costs for the forthcoming year), but you should get a firm estimate in writing of what these operating costs might be.

(b) Is it clear that your type of business will be permitted in the leased premises, and is there any prohibition on having an office that is open to the public? The part of the lease that refers to the type of business to be carried on in the premises should be as general as possible.

(c) What happens if, prior to the end of the term of the lease, the business is sold, moved elsewhere, or closed down? Leases generally have special provisions about your right to assign the lease or sublet part of your space in your lease to someone else, and this section should be reviewed very carefully.

(d) Is there a right of renewal? It is a common practice for a tenant to ask for a "right of renewal" provision in any lease, so that you (and not the landlord) have the option to renew the lease for a further term after the expiry of the initial term. These options to renew will have special time limits, and this section should be carefully reviewed by you and your lawyer.

(e) What are the insurance provisions? Every lease will have some kind of provision for insurance, whether you have to get your own insurance or pay part of the landlord's insurance. (Also note the other forms of insurance you will need, as previously discussed.)

Not only should you have all the insurance clauses in the proposed lease reviewed by your lawyer, but you should also give the whole lease to your insurance broker so he or she can make certain you have obtained all of the insurance required by your landlord.

Zoning Laws and Business Licenses

There are municipal regulations that you must take into consideration when you are starting a business. These regulations include zoning laws and a license to operate a business.

Zoning laws

Whether you lease your premises or are home based, check with the local authority (which may be a county, municipality, city, or even state or provincial authority) to ensure that your business can be legally carried out from the site. Many apartment buildings prohibit any kind of business. In some cases, you might even be prohibited from carrying on a special events business from your own single-family dwelling.

Land designations include agricultural, commercial, industrial, and residential. In most agricultural zones, home businesses can be operated with very few restrictions, and in commercial areas, the rule is generally to allow both commercial and residential activities. If you live in either of these zones, you can expect few if any problems.

Restrictions on the kind of business you can run from a home make sense. They are designed to protect neighborhoods from some of the more intrusive elements that can be a part of a business enterprise, such as odor, noise, excess traffic, and pollution. You may find other rules that severely limit your ability to operate, such as not being allowed to store inventory or employ anyone other than family members.

Licenses

You must be licensed to operate a business — it is the law. The licenses you need will vary among regions, but if you fail to obtain and pay the annual license fee, your local authorities may close down your business.

Check with city hall or your county clerk to see what the requirement is for your business. Your local chamber of commerce is also a source of information on permits and licenses.

Sales Taxes

In most states and provinces, you will be required to collect sales taxes on your services and to remit those monies to the appropriate taxing authority. It is important to register ahead of time and understand what records you must keep and how often you must file tax returns. You will need a sales tax number if your business buys goods for resale. This regulation applies in all states and provinces that have sales tax.

You will also likely pay some sales taxes on products that you buy, and it will be important to keep a separate record of all sales taxes you pay. In some jurisdictions, you can deduct the sales taxes you pay against the taxes you collect. In some places, you may be able to obtain an exemption from sales tax on your purchases (because you are a reseller of those products), but the exemption will require you to properly register ahead of time. A failure to pay sales taxes can be a serious crime.

In the United States, contact your state tax office, describe your business, and get the right permit.

Some jurisdictions charge taxes on services as well as taxes on products, and you must be sure to comply with the appropriate requirements. Most branches of government have booklets on the collection and remittance of sales and services taxes, which are usually available at no cost.

Canadian businesses must also collect and remit the goods and services tax (GST). Very few businesses are exempt from this tax, but if your annual revenue is less than a certain amount, you may fall under the "small trader" section. Contact your local Canada Revenue Agency office for details.

Employee-Related Regulations

If you plan to have full- or part-time employees, you should learn about any laws relating to employment standards, which may include a minimum hourly wage, holidays, hours of work, notice periods, etc. Even if an employee is prepared to break any of the mandatory employment rules, you should be aware that you might still be sued by this employee, or by the branch of government that looks after employees' rights, should you subsequently have to fire the employee or have any other kind of disagreement with him or her. The branch of government that handles employee rights will probably have a free booklet that will outline your basic responsibilities as an employer.

If you have one or more employees, you may be obligated to comply with statutory deductions specified by the tax department. This may include deduction and remittance of the employee's income tax, social services taxes, unemployment insurance tax, pension, etc.

You will need to register with the appropriate tax department as an employer; they likely have available a booklet that explains your obligations. Even if you are a one-person business, you may need to comply with certain tax obligations if you pay yourself a salary or dividends.

Many areas have compulsory requirements to register for workers' compensation or some other form of regulation relating to coverage of industrial accidents. Some places even require a one-person firm to register and to pay fees. A failure to properly register may result in fines or other costs relating to compensations if, for example, one of your employees is injured while on the job.

Miscellaneous Permits

You may or may not be required to comply with other permit requirements, including a permit to place a sign outside your premises, fire department permits, and health department permits. You should also ask your lawyer whether any other registration or permits are required to carry on your business.

A Final Word

Don't be put off by all of the above information on rules and regulations. Complying with them is not as difficult as it sounds. Your main objective is to make your proposed business legal from the beginning so that you will not have any unpleasant surprises in the future when you are busy producing events — and making money!

11
Accounting, Record Keeping, and Taxes

Although there is no typical special events business owner, those who work in this field are usually highly artistic people who prefer to focus on the creative side of the business. They often see record keeping, accounting, and tax concerns as unpleasant distractions from the main business of designing and producing events. You need to remember that you have started a business, not a hobby, and keeping accurate books and records is essential to your long-term success and profitability. Making sure you get all the tax deductions you are entitled to is just common sense.

Being organized and having a good bookkeeping system makes the job less unpleasant. Keeping your books current and accurate means you always have financial information immediately accessible.

You must keep up-to-date accounts, for tax departments require that you supply them with certain information and payments on a regular basis. Failing to file either federal or local government taxes can result in your company being fined or owing interest payments that can be easily avoided.

Knowing your exact financial position at all times also helps you determine your profitability and helps you make business decisions regarding incurring expenses, hiring employees, borrowing money, or expanding your operation. Because you are just starting out as a special events business, your operation will be small, and a simple manual accounting system is probably all that you need. You will find all the information and materials you need at any business stationery store. However, if you start out by investing in a computer-based accounting program, you will be prepared for growth and prosperity without having to revise your accounting processes along the way.

Accounting Software

In the past, computer-based accounting systems were too expensive and complex for most small businesses to operate. Today, dozens of accounting software programs are available to choose from, and that competition has made them affordable even to a small home-based special events business just starting out. Once you get over the initial hurdle of learning how to operate such a system, it will save you considerable time, money, and risk. While learning to keep company books on accounting software can be intimidating for most users, it is worth the time and trouble. The manuals are usually quite detailed and can make learning on your own difficult. That's why we recommend hiring a professional who can not only guide you through your purchase of accounting software, but who can also help you learn to use the system in a few short sessions.

Even business owners whose companies, like ours, have grown to the point where others are hired to do the books are wise to know how to use their accounting software. Being completely familiar with the accounting program allows you to access information at any time.

As mentioned, there are many affordable and effective accounting software packages on the market. Before you purchase one, do some research and make sure the program is going to work for you. If you purchase a new computer when starting up your business, that is the time to investigate accounting software packages. Consider hiring an experienced bookkeeper to help guide you through your purchase. This is especially important if you plan to hire a bookkeeper to help you later on.

If you already have a computer, you will need to purchase software that is compatible with your current equipment. One of today's most popular software packages is *Simply Accounting*. You can check out the program features online at <www.simplyaccounting.com>, or call ACCPAC Client Care at 1-800-773-5445 in Canada and the United States. You may also wish to explore software accounting packages specifically designed for the special events business. You will find a comprehensive list of products in the *Ultimate Technology Guide for Meeting Professionals*, by Corbin Ball, available to download free of charge at <www.mpiweb.org/resources/mpif/purchase.asp>.

Bookkeeping

In the early stages of business, you may do most of the bookkeeping yourself. Even so, hiring an experienced bookkeeper to set up a system and teach it to you can save you from a paper nightmare down the road. Additionally, you can then call this person to help you occasionally if your other work has taken precedence over keeping the books current. When your business has grown to the extent that you cannot handle the bookkeeping and office duties, hire a part-time bookkeeper to take over the job and increase his or her hours as the business warrants.

Get an accountant to handle the more complicated accounting functions and tax matters. If you keep accurate books, you should be able to give a hard copy and a computer disk to your accountant at year-end, and they will then prepare your year-end financial statements and tax returns.

Organize your time so that you are always up-to-date with your record keeping. Two to four hours per week (perhaps at the beginning or the end of the day) should be sufficient. It is essential to have current data regarding your business if you are going to make timely and wise decisions. If it looks like you are going to fall drastically behind in your bookkeeping, hire someone to come in and get the books current. It is a healthy sign if you are so busy working on events that you don't have the time to do bookkeeping. In this case, you should not hesitate to hire someone to help you out.

When you start out, you should create an opening balance sheet. See Sample 9 for an example of a balance sheet for a studio/office operation. The balance sheet provides you with a record of the business's assets, liabilities, and investments at the outset. We recommend that you prepare a balance sheet or "statement of condition" once a year. This is the yardstick by which you will measure your business growth. Your balance sheet allows you to calculate your business's net worth. It makes it possible to see at a glance whether you are making good progress toward your financial goals or need to rework your financial position by clearing off debt. In the beginning, you will likely create your own balance sheet, but as your business grows, you may want to give this duty to an accountant. Just remember that this is your business, and to help it prosper, you should always be intimately aware of your bottom line.

Accounts Receivable

Even if you don't have a specialized business or accounting program, you will find it simple and convenient to have an invoice template on file in your company computer. See Sample 4 in chapter 7 for an example of an invoice. After designing an initial template on your computer, you should always save changes when generating a new invoice. Doing this allows you to track the number sequence and simply type over the data you need to change. Make sure you have the correct accounts payable contact information along with the preferred method for receiving invoices, such as by fax, e-mail, or hard copy through the mail. Send the original to the customer and retain one copy for your records. Keep file copies of invoices in a three-ring binder in numerical order and by month of transaction. Start a new binder for each fiscal year of your business. You may also find it helpful to include a copy in the client file. When you receive payment, remember to stamp the invoice paid.

Set a designated time to enter accounts receivable and paid invoices into your computer accounting system. You could schedule this duty on a weekly, bi-weekly, or monthly basis. Whenever you decide to schedule time to do computer data entry, make sure you will not be distracted by the phone or other interruptions, for this task requires a high level of concentration.

Invoices should be kept under the heading "Accounts Receivable" on your accounting system. If the data is kept current, you will have a complete list of your clients, along with a contact name, address, and phone and fax numbers. Your receivables account will also provide the total revenue for the month as well as any taxes paid. Keeping your books current by entering data regularly makes it easy to monitor how much money you owe the government and what money is owed to you by clients.

SAMPLE 9
BALANCE SHEET

XYZ Events (studio/office operation)
OPENING BALANCE SHEET
AS AT _____, 20-

ASSETS:

Petty cash	$50
Monies in bank	2,000
Accounts receivable	0
Deposits	500
Prepaid expenses	1,300
Furniture and equipment	1,825
Computers and printer	4,000
TOTAL ASSETS	**$9,675**

LIABILITIES:

Sales tax payable	$0
Federal taxes payable	0
Accounts payable	4,000
Employee benefits payable	0
Wages payable	0
Monies owed to bank/investors	0

EQUITY:

Owner's investment in company	$5,675
Net profit/loss to date	0
TOTAL LIABILITIES AND EQUITY	**$9,675**

Keep in mind that not declaring all sources of income from your business is tax fraud and can carry heavy fines as well as destroy your company's reputation if the information becomes public.

Accounts Payable

As important as it is to keep track of the money owed to you, you will find it equally important to monitor the money you owe to others. You'll find as a special events business that you have many out-of-pocket expenses tied to your operations and your events. If you start out with a good system for keeping track of your spending, you will avoid the mistakes that send other event specialists into the red. This section provides you with some sound advice for dealing with the following elements of accounts payable:

(a) Petty cash

(b) COD and cash purchases

(c) Payable invoices

(d) Company credit cards

(e) Personally paid company expenses

Petty cash

Write a check to your bank for petty cash ranging from $100 to $200 and keep that money in a locked box or drawer to use for last-minute or incidental expenses. Buy a book of petty cash receipts and attach the sales slip from your purchases to the receipt. Write enough information on the form so you will know what expense account number it should go to when doing your computer accounting.

When the petty cash is almost gone, write another check to bring the amount up to the petty cash float you have decided to maintain. File the petty cash receipts in numerical order by month.

COD and cash purchases

As a new special events business, you will be paying cash for many of your initial supplies and services rather than having accounts and being billed by suppliers, in which case you would be keeping track of accounts payable through your invoices. With cash receipts, it is very important to identify the purpose of the purchase on the receipt and file it as soon as possible. Looking at cash receipts without a clue as to which account they belong is like throwing money away.

Where possible, use a company check for purchases and always keep a copy of the invoice or sales receipt. Stamp your copy of the receipt paid, and write on it the date of payment, the check number, and the expense account or event to which it refers. Place all paid receipts in a file for the month in which they were paid, after entering the data into your computer accounting system. (Ensure you also stamp them as entered.) File them either alphabetically, by supplier or client, or by event. You will want to have easy access to these receipts for repeat orders or to look up a cost or quantity you previously ordered.

Payable invoices

When you have set up an account with a supplier, you will receive invoices with the terms of payment. The terms will vary depending on the type of account and supplier. Your telephone company will expect the bill to be paid by a specific date. A caterer may give you 30 days. Paying your bills on time is essential to your long-term credit rating.

When you write a check for the invoice, mark it paid and write the date, check number, and expense account or event account on your file copy. File the invoices accordingly, and enter the data in your computer accounting system. Mark the invoices as having been entered and file them for easy future access.

Company credit cards

Having a credit card that you use solely for company business will help streamline your accounting and bookkeeping. There will be certain instances when paying with a credit card is your only option. It will be much less complicated if you use a credit card designated for business purchases only. Treat the bill the way you would any other payable invoice. Using a credit card is the preferred method for paying for business travel and entertaining clients.

Keep good records if you intend to deduct these expenses from your income. Write as much information as possible on the back of your credit card receipt about the meeting or reason for the expense. Your accountant will be able to tell you what your allowable deduction is for travel and entertainment expenses.

Personally paid company expenses

Purchase a book of employee expense account forms at your local stationery store. Use these forms for recording any out-of-pocket expenses you or any employees may incur. Make sure these expense reports are kept up-to-date and done every month.

Whenever possible, a receipt should be attached to the report; however, there are occasions when small amounts for items such as parking meters, gratuities, or automobile expenses may be reported without receipt backup. Write a company check to yourself or to your employees for the amount owing, record the date and check number on the expense form, and file it for input into the accounting system for the month that it pertains to.

Keep these expense reports filed in a separate place by month and by year. This is the type of backup material you would be required to produce if your company was ever to be audited by the tax department. For example, both the IRS and Canada Revenue Agency require that all vehicle expenses be recorded and kept. In the special events business, your vehicle costs can add up quickly; however, you must keep track of the entire year's expenses, including fuel, repairs, insurance, parking, depreciation, interest on the vehicle loan, and licensing and registration fees. If you use your vehicle for both business and pleasure, allocate the expense to your business based on a percentage of business to pleasure use. Your accountant will be able to help you correctly allocate vehicle expenses to your business.

Payroll

If your company is incorporated or if you have employees, you are responsible for deductions at source from your employees' wages or salaries. You must open an account with your local tax department. You will be assigned a number and will receive a book of tables to use as a reference for the deductions you must make each month and the portion you are required to pay for unemployment insurance or government pension plans.

Read the information carefully and phone or meet with a tax department representative if you have questions or are unsure of your responsibilities as an employer. To avoid penalties, you must file on time and correctly with any government entity. Your computer accounting system will have a separate heading called payroll, and all payments and information regarding employment will be entered there. Here is another good reason to hire an experienced bookkeeper: to show you all you need to know regarding the use of the payroll account. You need to keep accurate payroll records in the event of any kind of dispute between you and a current or former employee.

Inventory

Beyond the basics, a computer-based accounting program is a helpful tool for tracking inventory. Entering inventory purchases correctly into the computer saves time and provides you with easy access to your financial situation. Every special events business is different in terms of the inventory they carry. When you are starting out, you will find it more advantageous financially to rent equipment or display items than to purchase them. Make an investment only when you find yourself renting the same equipment or display items over and over (such as easels, ballot boxes, display stands, signage pedestals, or décor items).

Maximizing Deductible Expenses

Every successful business needs to keep track of any tax-deductible expenses. Expenses are allowed if they are related to the operation of the business, are reasonable, ordinary and necessary, and if they are for items to be used within a period of one year. Your accountant can advise you in your particular situation.

If you are going to incur expenses that would be useful for more than one year, generally that expense cannot be fully deducted within the year the money is spent. The depreciation formula for these expenses, or capital assets, such as computers, desks, automobiles, etc., may be claimed for the useful life of the asset.

One of the main advantages of running a home-based special events business is your right to deduct a certain portion of your home expenses, such as heat, rent, taxes, utilities, and mortgage. To take advantage of these deductions, you must prove that you use a specific area of your home solely for the purpose of running your business. You cannot claim deductions for an office or workshop that also occupies a part of your kitchen or bedroom. Your accountant will be able to advise you as to what deductions are legal in your area. To ensure that you account for all expenses, keep all payment stubs, receipts, and vouchers, and maintain a record of entertainment and automobile expenses. The tax department can disallow claims for expenses if they are not verified.

Some of the areas you should discuss with your accountant are —

- home office (if applicable),
- automobile,
- entertainment,
- travel,
- bad debts,
- insurance,
- education and professional development,
- business association memberships,
- salaries (if you employ family members),
- equipment,
- furnishings, and
- interest.

It is critical that you receive expert tax advice in advance on these and other expense deductions related to your business. Tax regulations and interpretations change frequently. Only a tax accountant can properly advise you on the appropriate deductions in your situation.

Accountants

Do not rely on the advice of a bookkeeper when the time comes to file and pay your year-end taxes. Seek the advice and services of a professional accountant, who can advise you on how to minimize taxes payable and maximize your profits according to current rules and regulations. Again, tax rules and regulations are highly complex, vary according to your business location, and are subject to change.

Trying to look after your own business accounting with no outside assistance is like trying to be your own doctor or lawyer. This is one of the times when you must pay for the advice and services of a professional.

You can save your accountant time and yourself money, however, by keeping your books up-to-date and your records organized. Also, seek the services of a good accountant by asking your lawyer, bank manager, or other business owners for the names of several reputable accountants. Large accounting firms can be expensive and may be unfamiliar with the operations of small businesses. An accountant in a small- to medium-size firm will be more affordable and will also have a greater understanding of your business.

Do not hesitate to interview several people before making your choice, and ask up front about what kind of fees you should expect. A long-term relationship with an accountant can be very rewarding to your business, so hire someone you relate to on a personal level and who can explain financial information in plain language.

12
Developing Your Portfolio

As a special events company, you need to develop a professional portfolio to showcase your work to prospective clients. Your portfolio will show a potential client tangible evidence of your work as well as allow you to demonstrate your creative and stylistic abilities. It is an opportunity to sell your business and promote your brand. Without a well-organized and artistic portfolio, you will be selling your services on your word alone. The special events business can be extremely competitive, and a lax approach to your portfolio will lose you business. With a little money and time, you can develop a very impressive portfolio. This chapter shows you how.

Building Your First Portfolio

When you are starting out, you won't have much to work with. But you can still start preparing for your portfolio by creating your own events. If your business will be as a wedding planner, you can create your first event without a real wedding. Plan the event step-by-step. Make a hard copy of the wedding plan and the critical path (see chapter 13). Include these in your portfolio. Draft a complete budget that itemizes all the expenses in your "wedding." Create another document that lists three types of weddings and gives ballpark costs.

Consider renting a tuxedo and wedding gown for the day and having friends pose for photographs you can include. Or simply take some photographs of the venues and locations to be used in your wedding plans. Design the invitations or purchase samples of paper. Include swatches of fabric to demonstrate the color scheme. Talk to caterers or do some research on the internet to find interesting recipes to include in your portfolio. Include a sample menu. Put your portfolio in order, from the initial planning through the event itself. Ensure that you have adequate samples and illustrations to give your verbal presentation an even flow.

Maintaining a Professional Portfolio

As you begin to work on real events, start to collect a range of items to showcase your event experience. Collect photographs of your events as well as testimonials from satisfied clients and event participants, plus any media clippings that demonstrate your success. Make sure you get copies of brochures and other marketing collateral developed for the event. Get permission from clients to use plans and other documentation that shows the type of work you do. If your client isn't comfortable sharing this information, you can explain the absence of any elements when presenting the other items in your portfolio.

Every client is different. Some may require that you sign a confidentiality or intellectual property agreement where any and all information created belongs to the client. It is important to discuss your plans to use information in your portfolio with each client. Most will be comfortable with your using photographs and public documents such as brochures later in your portfolio, whereas event plans and budgets are more likely to be kept confidential. Ensure that you have your client's permission, and be specific about the manner in which you plan on using the information or materials in future. Respecting your existing client's wishes is far more important than taking a risk by showing something that could compromise your relationship.

Keep all items in good shape by placing them in plastic sheets in a binder. Use tabs so that it is easy to flip from one event to another. A professional portfolio should be kept up-to-date, clean, in good shape, and to a maximum of about 20 pages.

Types of Portfolios

You may choose to utilize part of your company website as a portfolio. You can also keep an electronic version of your portfolio on CD-ROM. However, neither a CD-ROM nor a web portfolio should take the place of a physical version. Having an electronic portfolio shows potential clients that you are comfortable with technology and provides them with additional and ready access to your samples and achievements. You can refer to this during your interview with a client or in a presentation, but do not miss the opportunity to showcase your work to a ready audience. After all, you have no guarantee that a potential client will actually go to your website or look at your CD-ROM after you have left.

Creating a physical portfolio can be costly, depending on which presentation method you choose. The standard portfolio is a simple binder with clear plastic pockets or sleeves for storing brochures, invitations, mini-posters, media clippings, advertisements, and testimonials as well as photographs. You can keep these items loose within the sleeves, or you can buy a specialized portfolio binder with larger plastic pockets that allow enough room to include card stock. Experiment and use your creativity. Mount your photos and portfolio documents on black card in an artistic fashion. Use captions with your photographs, and mix up horizontal and vertical presentation.

Bristol board is a good durable choice, as is mat board, which is heavier. If there is no portfolio supply store near you, most stationery stores and art supply stores will carry portfolio cases or the items you need to create a professional-looking portfolio. You can also find some great supplies on the internet, but it would be wise to get personal assistance to begin with. Costs start at about $100.

You will also need a method for transporting your portfolio. A wide array of choices exists, ranging from a simple zipper case to an aluminum attaché. Of course, the costs can range just as dramatically. As a new special events business, you will want to try to keep your costs to a minimum and choose something attractive yet practical.

Presenting Your Portfolio

Your portfolio is the visual documentary of your events. It must be relevant to the contract you are bidding on. Tailor it to the goals and objectives (see chapter 13) of each potential client and project. You should try to demonstrate similar events your company has produced and the particular skills, knowledge, and creativity used to make each a success. It should not overwhelm the client with extra material that is neither relevant nor supported by the successful details of your event. Two to three pages per event should be enough. Some events will require less space, some more, depending on the nature of the event. Remember, the portfolio is a visual medium, so do not include anything that doesn't have a physical appeal.

You should give as much care and consideration to the manner in which you present your portfolio as you did to the methods you used to prepare it. Simply passing around your portfolio to clients will lose you points in your presentation. Tell a story using your samples, and make sure you can support the evidence with hard statistics such as numbers of participants and ticket sales.

13
The Event Planning Process

From the outside, the special events business appears to be based on creativity and energy. While that is true, a successful event cannot be achieved by creativity alone. The reason event planning has grown steadily over the years as its own industry is due in large part to the complexity of planning and executing events. Although creativity is an important element that can foster a memorable event, it is the care and attention given to the details that makes an event successful from start to finish. This chapter will help guide you through the critical elements of event planning, which are key to building a successful event and a solid reputation as a special events professional.

The Event Plan

Every successful event starts with a plan. Regardless of whether you are planning a wedding with 200 guests or a three-day trade show with thousands of attendees, you need to begin with a sound strategy that identifies every element of the event. The plan helps you create effective schedules; project costs that will keep you within your budget and still make you a profit; assign tasks and responsibilities; and identify and anticipate potential trouble areas.

If you don't have a specific event to work on at this time, you can use this chapter as an exercise. Read through it now with a "mock" event in mind and refer back to it when the time comes to plan your first real event.

Background Information

The background section of the plan includes details you have gathered about the project so far. Some of this information may be outlined in an RFP (request for proposals). See chapter 15 for more on the RFP process. It is in your best interest to know these basic details before you sign a contract. For the purpose of this chapter, let's assume you have a project and a client to work with, and begin with your client meeting.

Try to avoid going to your first client meeting with dozens of your own ideas. Your first step is to listen. Ultimately, this is your client's event, not yours. You want to deliver the goals that your client has in mind, and you won't get to know those if you come armed with your own plans. Even the most disorganized client will most likely know what the end goal should be. Go to your first meeting with a notepad and pen, and take good, detailed notes. Ask questions. Your client will likely have specific information to give you. If not, you can get details by asking about —

- the reason for the event (or vision),

- the date of the event (approximate or set),

- the number of guests (invited or targeted), and

- the budget (or your fee).

You may get further details from this meeting, such as the history of the event. Although asking questions can be helpful, try not to trouble your client with too many. Listening is the key, but if the answers don't come, better to ask than to leave without direction after the meeting has ended. Ask questions that can help you provide a better event, but only ask as the details flow. These kinds of questions might include the following:

- Has the event been held before?

- Who worked on it?

- Was it successful?

- What kinds of problems were there, if any?

- Has the budget been altered? Why?

- What kind of feedback did the event receive?

- Was there any follow-up to measure success?

- Is any of that information available to you?

Use this information as your background material. Fill in as many details in the overall section as you can now. Based on this information, you will further develop your plan.

Goals and Objectives

Every successful event needs to have its goals and its objectives identified at the start of the planning process. A goal is the overall desired result that the client wishes to achieve. The objectives are specific targets that need to be met in order to realize the goal. For example, the goal of a corporate awards banquet might tie to a corporate strategy of receiving recognition as one of the Top 100 employers. Or the event might be a fund-raiser, with the goal to raise a certain amount of money.

Identifying the goals will help you set the specific objectives that must be met. A common way of setting objectives is to use the SMART method, in which SMART is an acronym for Specific, Measurable, Achievable, Realistic, and Time-bound. This method examines whether an objective is a valid and mutually accepted benchmark in achieving the desired result. Here are instructions for applying the SMART test to set objectives:

- *Specific:* Frame objectives starting with the word "to," as in the following examples: to raise awareness of a new association; to raise $750,000 in funds; to promote a sense of community.

- *Measurable:* Depending on the type of event, define methods to measure success. Many objectives have clear methods of measurement, while others are less tangible. For an awareness-building event, you can measure awareness through media monitoring. (Did the event get media coverage?) You can seek industry commentary by reviewing corporate or association newsletters. (Ask participants to reference the event, then monitor their responses.) You can also ask for quotes from participants. When they are positive, they are great to include in your portfolio and to use in marketing the event in the future.

For a conference or trade show, you should always provide a questionnaire inviting participants' feedback. If you develop a questionnaire or evaluation form, be as thorough as possible so you can easily determine what to keep and what to work on. To ensure consistency in the responses, offer check boxes for poor, fair, good, and excellent, then allow for a section on comments.

Timing of evaluation is critical; evaluations given at the site will bring in the freshest commentary. If you can't evaluate the participants on site, offer the participants an easy method for follow-up. A web-based or e-mail evaluation form is easy to provide and costs less than for a mail-out. You might also see if your client is willing to sponsor a follow-up luncheon meeting with key participants to brainstorm on the pros and cons of the event.

The main thing to remember when measuring results is to be clear — you need to tie measurement to each objective. This is how you will sell your services in the future, by demonstrating that you met the event's objectives.

- *Achievable:* You should not try to achieve more than is actually possible. Tasks often take longer and require more work than originally anticipated. If the objective appears too big to start with, chances are that it will be very tough to achieve.

- *Realistic:* Much like the achievable test, you need to know if an objective is attainable. Examine the resources available, both human and financial. It is better to identify whether an objective is really necessary to reach the end goal than to invest much time and effort into meeting a not-so-important target. Look at the risks of dropping an objective against the benefits of meeting it. Discuss the implications with your client — even if you disagree, you do need to respect the client's wishes.

- *Time-bound:* Define the boundaries of meeting each objective. How long will it take to meet the objective and where does it fit into the overall plan? Make sure you examine this carefully, for it will relate to an objective being both achievable and reasonable.

In summary, the objectives answer the question of why the client is holding an event. Depending on the size of the project, you might be able to share these with your client at the first meeting.

However, even with small events, you will be better off writing the objectives down and sharing them with your client after the initial meeting. Do a follow-up letter outlining the goals and objectives of the event as discussed in the meeting, and ask for comments. You need to have it in writing that your client agrees to the stated targets and the resources tied to them. This will provide more detailed information than is in your contract.

Agenda

How will the event you are planning actually unfold? The agenda is the all-important minute-by-minute schedule of the structure of the event. It is the document from which everything else is determined: rentals, audiovisuals, decorations, food and beverage, entertainment, signage, etc. Much of what ends up in the final agenda is determined as planning proceeds. However, it is vital to begin with an outline of your event before you can move to the budgeting phase; otherwise, how will you know what you are budgeting for?

Think through the event in detail. What will be happening and in what sequence? Have you left time for attendees to mingle? Have you scheduled coffee and lunch breaks? Do you need entertainment as part of your agenda? Avoid gaps in time, and ensure all key players know where they are to be and when. A well-thought-out agenda will ensure a memorable event.

Venue

Quite simply, without a venue, there is no event. And without a venue that matches the event style (wedding, meeting, awards banquet, fund-raiser, etc.), you put the success of your event at risk. Given the importance of ensuring the right venue for your event, the choice needs to be made up front, once goals and objectives have been identified.

Although the idea of selecting a venue seems straightforward, plenty of details need to be considered in finding the best space for your event. From your first client meeting, you should have a good idea of your site selection requirements. Space is the leading consideration. How many people will be expected or are desired at the event? Find out the maximum number of expected participants and go from there. From the set objectives, you should be able to determine what special considerations need to be accommodated. Detail these, and when you make your calls to the contacts for the venue, find out if the space will accommodate your event needs. Here are just a few of the details you may need to consider in selecting your site:

(a) Remember that location matters. When choosing a location, think about the event participants and their transportation to and from the event. (Airport access may be necessary.)

(b) Determine whether the "look" of the facility makes a difference to the success of the event (e.g., oceanside or downtown? artsy or high-tech?).

(c) Access to the facility is very important. Find out when you can begin to set up and when you have to clear out, whether you can store materials for early deliveries, what kind of security and insurance the venue offers (for auction items and other expensive materials), and whether the building has freight and wheelchair access.

(d) Access to power is important too. Make sure that the space has adequate outlets and the right lighting and layout for presentation and audiovisual needs.

(e) Find out if they offer extra rooms for staff/volunteers to take breaks and gather.

(f) Check whether the venue has a business centre or production office.

(g) Consider what role weather might play in the choice of location. For instance, is the venue heated and/or air conditioned? Is there a porte cochere in case of rain? Will rain or ice make it dangerous for participants to get to the venue?

(h) Find out if parking is accessible and whether it is available free or at cost to participants.

(i) If the event is more than one day, there should be other services and amenities nearby for quick excursions, such as shopping or sightseeing.

(j) If your event will include VIPs or celebrities, you should look for a site with a separate, private entrance and exit or one that provides a smaller VIP room.

(k) Find out what other services are provided by the venue, such as registration, audiovisual, staffing, catering, or bar and beverage service.

(l) Ask about attrition and cancellation policies.

Never commit to a venue without doing a site inspection first. You need to see the site in advance before making your reservation. Don't delay in sourcing your venue, as good venues book up quickly. Be imaginative and strategic. Every city has a number of standard venues for events. Hotels, convention centers, universities and colleges, airports, and community centers all have meeting rooms or a larger facility, if that's what your event calls for. Good facilities may also be found at museums, art galleries, or restaurants.

If your event calls for creativity, make sure you think of all possible sites. Of course, your location must also fit within your budget. The next section introduces the basic elements of planning an event budget. See chapter 14 for more information on selecting venues.

Budget

Just as an architect needs a blueprint to build a structure, an event professional needs a blueprint to build an event. The budget is your blueprint as an event professional, defining how you will meet your goals and objectives. Before you begin your budget planning, ask yourself these questions: Is your client trying to make money from this event? Is your client covering all expenses or are you trying to break even? The answers to these questions will determine whether you want high-end products and services or whether you need to scale down in your planning.

First, make a list of all anticipated expenses. See Worksheet 6 for a list of typical expenses found in event budgets. Of course, you will need to tailor this list to fit your event. As you can see, working from your agenda helps you decide what to include as expenses in your budget.

Some costs will be fixed and will not change with the number of participants. Fixed costs include elements such as audiovisual equipment, power, décor, venue and room rental as well as insurance, signage, entertainment, and associated travel and per diems. However, even fixed costs can become variable if the number of participants increases substantially, requiring you to add labor or space and décor. Variable costs are those that are dependent on the number of participants, such as food and beverage, giveaways, accommodations, registration, and staffing.

WORKSHEET 6
EVENT BUDGET

REVENUE	Amount	$/per	Estimate	Actual	Comments
Ticket Sales					
Sponsorship					
EXPENSES					
Item	**Amount**	**$/per**	**Estimate**	**Actual**	**Comments**
Event Insurance/Licensing/Permits					
Venue or Room Rental					
Valet Parking					
Security					
Coat Check Labor					
Entrance Area					
Décor					
- flowers/fabric/props/room décor					
Décor Labor					
Lighting					
Audio					
Audiovisual					
Entertainment/Greeters					
Power					
Reception Area					
Food and Beverage					
- cocktails/wine					
- liquor tax on alcohol					
- hors d'oeuvres					
- service charge/gratuities					
Décor					
- flowers/fabric/props/room decor					
- table linens					
- table decor					
- candles/holders					

Item	Amount	$/per	Estimate	Actual	Comments
Décor Labor					
Lighting					
Audio					
Audiovisual					
Entertainment/Greeters					
Power					
Main Ballroom					
Food and Beverage					
- cocktails/wine					
- liquor tax on alcohol					
- dinner/dessert					
- coffee/cappuccino bar					
- additional bartender labor					
- additional chef's labor					
- service charge/gratuities					
Staging					
- set design/props					
- risers					
- podium					
Pipe and Drape					
Décor					
- table linens					
- napkins					
- table centerpieces					
- table accessories					
- candles/holders					
- chairs/covers					
- room decor					
Décor Labor					
Lighting					

Item	Amount	$/per	Estimate	Actual	Comments
Audio					
Audiovisual					
Entertainment/Greeters					
Power					
Additional Entertainment Expenses					
- per diems/meals for entertainers					
- accommodation for entertainers					
- transportation rentals/mileage					
Miscellaneous Expenses					
Event Management Staff					
- production manager					
- technical manager					
- carpenters/misc. labor					
- general event labor					
- radios for communication					
Rental Deliveries/Trucking					
Décor Deliveries/Trucking					
Music Union Dues					
Crew Costs					
- crew meals					
- crew accommodations					
- crew parking					
Estimated Summary of Expenses before Taxes					
Plus applicable taxes					
Contingency on all	5%–10%				
Estimated Subtotal of Expenses					
Event Management Fee					
Plus applicable taxes					
Total Estimated Expenses					

In Worksheet 6, the "Amount" column is the number required, the "$ / per" is the cost per person, and the "Estimate" is the expected total cost. You will not need to use each column for every category listed. For example, for audiovisual, you will not need to break down the costs per participant. You will only require an estimate and an actual cost. With food and beverage, you *will* need to know the costs per person. Feel free to expand the "Comments" column. (This is where you can add notes, such as a lower cost that is offered with a commitment to a specific quantity.)

You will also need to include revenue in your budget, whether it comes from one source or a number of sources. Some of these sources include registration fees, ticket sales, sponsorships, and in-kind donations.

To determine how much you will require in revenues to either break even or make a profit, add up all fixed and variable costs. Divide this figure by the number of expected participants to set your registration fees or ticket price. If the amount is more than your budget allows, you will then know whether to reduce expenses, seek sponsorships, increase the registration fee, or increase paid attendance. Your event management fee may be a fixed cost for events such as weddings that do not generate revenues, in which case your budget need only break even. However, if your fee is based on profits, you will need to apply a formula to ensure that your costs are covered in the budget. Whichever method you are using, make sure that you have adequately accounted for your payment in setting and sticking to your budget. For more information on covering your payment in the budget, see chapter 5.

When you use your agenda as a starting point and break down the venue into its respective rooms, creating a budget isn't really as hard as it might appear. Like developing a critical path (discussed in the next section), it's time-consuming but very necessary. A key piece of advice: put every expense and revenue item into your budget and keep it updated. Expenses can add up quickly!

Critical Path

A critical path, also called a timeline or "workback," schedules the component activities of an event plan, determining the minimum amount of time required for each. No matter what you wish to call it, this piece in the planning process is vital to your sanity — and to your event's success. A good critical path will keep you on track, identifying what needs to be done and by what date. It will ensure that nothing falls through the cracks on your way to event day.

A critical path will differ from event to event, depending on the size of the event, what kind it is, and whether you have a planning team. Broad activities to include in a critical path include the following:

- Define goals and objectives.
- Map out a draft agenda.
- Research and book venues.
- Book speakers.
- Develop a marketing and PR plan.
- Establish registration procedure.
- Design and send out invitations.
- Plan staffing and/or volunteer services.
- Secure donations for a silent or live auction.
- Plan food and beverage needs.
- Decide on audiovisual needs.
- Research any license requirements.
- Plan media involvement.
- Book entertainment.
- Plan decorations.
- Meet regularly with site staff.
- Follow up with thank-you letters, evaluation, media survey, etc.

You may need to take larger aspects of the critical path and break them out into their own detailed action plans. An action plan is a detailed schedule of the steps and time frames needed for carrying out a very specific element tied to an event. Breaking one particular element out into its own action plan allows you to provide the schedule to the specific individuals who are doing the work. It also keeps the critical path focused on the main aspects of the event. For example, an action plan for media involvement could include the following steps:

(a) Identify spokesperson.

(b) Develop list of target media.

(c) Determine publication deadlines for print media.

(d) Determine availability of VIPs or celebrities for interviews.

(e) Develop written materials such as press release, media advisory, and speaking notes. Each will require separate time frames for drafts, revisions, and sign-off.

(f) Issue press release. Plan to issue this as close to the event as possible, but also to meet publication deadlines.

(g) Issue media advisory (one day prior).

Sometimes it's easier to create your critical path and action plans in reverse order, working backwards from the day of the event to the present. Figure out when you must have something completed and then decide how much time is needed to complete that task. It is important to remember to build in some extra time so you are not panicking on the day of your event because you are still waiting for materials from the printer. You may find it takes quite a bit of time to create a critical path, but we know from experience that you will feel confident about staying on top of the details after taking this step.

Audience

Event Planning 101: Know Your Audience. Who are they? Where are they coming from? Why will they want to come to your event? How will you keep them interested? And how will you make them want to come next time? These are all questions to ask yourself when planning an event. If you don't know your audience and have some idea of their expectations, you risk fatal errors in planning. Get well acquainted with the tastes of your audience: you do not want to be serving beer and nuts to a champagne and caviar crowd, or vice versa. Although you may not hear complaints at the time of the event, you won't get their business again.

Once you know who your target audience is, you need to take into account the following considerations, among others.

Invitations

To get attendees at your event, invitations can be as simple as an e-mail note to members of an association or as fancy as mailed-out, printed invitations. Whichever way works for your event, remember to factor in any costs attached and to ensure you have a system for recording confirmed attendees.

Registration

Larger events generally require attendees to register for the event rather than simply respond to an invitation. Attendees may need to select workshops or indicate food preferences. You need to decide what information to collect, what payment options to make available, and how you will provide information to attendees on social events, family options, directions, or attire. Generally, attendees register electronically through a registration management system. Remember to plan staffing for an on-site registration booth where attendees can pick up their registration packages and their name tags.

Transportation and accommodation

Your audience will need to know how to get to your event and where they can stay. In most cases, attendees are responsible for their own transportation and accommodation, but it is up to your special events business to communicate the available options. With electronic tools at our disposal, this task is considerably easier than in the past. If your event has a website to which you can direct attendees, this is one easy way to share information. Another option, if available, is to send an e-mail to all attendees including this information. Remember to collect e-mail addresses from registrants if you want to send out information this way. Also consider your audience and whether all will have ready access to the internet or an e-mail account.

Partners/Kids

Depending on the size of your event and whether it is drawing people from out of town, you may wish to include activities for spouses or children who have come along with the event attendee. Just a few of the examples of items to consider are a museum visit, recreational activity, or city tour. If your partner activities are successful, those that came along may insist that everyone attends again the next year. And you will earn that many more referrals to your special events business!

Speakers

Your client may already have decided who they would like to speak at the event or meeting. It could be a CEO, company president, or a particular motivational speaker they like. Larger events usually have at least one keynote speaker as well as several workshop sessions.

The choice of speakers is critical to the success of your event. The right speakers set the tone, motivate the audience, and can determine whether people will participate next time. If you are organizing guest speakers for your client or are asked for your recommendations, several speakers bureaus can be found on the web to assist you in your search. Proceed with caution. Popular speakers are not free and can take a big bite out of your budget. On the other hand, they can also help ensure a large audience at your event.

Takeaways

Similar to gift bags at children's birthday parties, takeaways have become a happy expectation at meetings and events. Whether it's a tote bag, highlighter, fridge magnet, or key chain, takeaways serve to provide good memories of your event, especially if the items are useful. Promotional companies have catalogues with pages and pages of ideas; many are also available on websites. You may want to consider takeaways that add to your event's theme.

Baseball hats and T-shirts with logos are standard takeaways for sporting events. Less ordinary would be golf balls with the logo or the name of the event. Corporate events might include such takeaways as card holders, mugs, or tote bags. Remember, the more useful or fun the item, the more likely it will be used and appreciated as well as seen. Often you will find that companies are happy to donate items if their logos or names will be used as well.

Decide how these items should be distributed: at the registration desk, on chairs in meeting rooms, during meals, or in hotel rooms. Planning takeaways is a fun part of event planning — be creative.

Partners and Sponsors

As you begin to work with different clients and gain experience in the world of event planning, you will discover how many players can be involved in just one event. Among the groups you will need to work with are volunteers, the media, and sponsors. These groups will provide additional support to events while saving you and your clients the hard costs that would otherwise be involved in hiring their services. This section introduces the kinds of assistance such groups provide as well as tips on how to gain their support. The more you can offer when meeting with a client in terms of added value, the more clients you will find yourself gaining over time.

Volunteers

Volunteers for your special events can fill in just about anywhere — from a professional copywriter to help you produce written materials for your event to an entire group that will assist in staffing on event day. Volunteers have personal reasons for being involved in an event. If you are producing an event for a nonprofit agency, you will likely have access to a list of regular volunteers. Ask for assistance from those in the agency who have worked with the volunteers in the past. Other places you might look for volunteer help are your local colleges or universities. Seek out students in related fields such as hospitality or in the relevant sector, should you be organizing an event for life sciences or biotechnology. Volunteering provides students with some hands-on experience and good networking opportunities, so pitch these benefits when you advertise for helpers. To find these volunteers, try posting notices on physical and electronic job boards or student listservs.

Be careful, though, to educate your volunteers about what is within the bounds of appropriate behavior in addressing the event participants. This can be especially tricky if you are working on an event that celebrities will be attending. Although finding volunteers for such an event can be easy, you need to be clear that it is not an opportunity for harassing the guests! Other sources of volunteers are service clubs, whose members might volunteer their time in exchange for a donation to their association.

Media

As a special events business, you should become very familiar with your local media. These include your local TV stations (whether independent or local affiliates), local community television, local radio stations, and daily and community newspapers. (See chapter 8 for more tips on working with the media.) Often newspapers have a column or section for upcoming events. If you want to sell tickets to your event, get the information in there!

If you are working with a nonprofit organization, they may have existing relationships with local media that can provide extra value to your event. This could include time and costs from the community or local TV station to film a video of the people who have benefited from the charity, which can be shown at the event. It might be a story in the local paper or an interview with one of the event's celebrities on TV or radio to raise the profile of the event, supporting ticket sales or registration. In exchange for volunteer time and costs, the local media will get its name listed on event materials such as the brochure, website, event signage, and thank-you letters. Be media friendly and see what can result from it.

Sponsors

Like help from the media, sponsorship is a great way to add value to your event without assuming the extra costs. Talk to your client to try to identify potential sponsors. These can be approached for formal sponsorship, such as at a corporate conference where partners provide value in exchange for benefits associated with the event. If you specialize in soliciting sponsors, your special events business can gain an excellent reputation.

Corporations and governments face tighter budgets as competition and costs grow. They are looking for every opportunity to share or offset costs by partnering with other organizations to add value to their projects. At the same time, both corporations and governments are often expected to contribute to certain associations' events and will be conspicuous by their absence if they do not participate. Familiarize yourself with other special events to see how they solicit sponsorships. Again, the internet can provide you with some excellent examples of sponsorship requests for different types of events. There are often different levels of sponsorship. Typically, these would be bronze, silver, gold, and platinum; however, some events tailor the names to fit the theme of the event.

Plan carefully and plan early regarding sponsorships. Like the media and volunteers, your sponsors want to benefit from the experience. Whether that benefit is greater access to your client (or the event participants) or the potential exposure of having their names listed as sponsors, you need to develop a desirable package that encourages participation. And a final word of caution: be flexible in what you offer, but be consistent. You do not want to elicit bad feelings among your sponsors by playing favorites.

Marketing

How are you going to get people to come to your meeting, fundraiser, or gala event? The answer is by marketing your event. By using effective marketing tools, you can show why people will want to attend your event. You must highlight your goals and objectives and demonstrate the benefits to the audience. We all want to know what's in it for us, what's going to make us change our routines and possibly spend money.

Before beginning any marketing plan, you must know two things: who your potential audience is and how much money you can spend to reach them. Here are some marketing ideas:

- Newspaper ads
- Brochures
- Radio ads
- Trade publication ads
- Flyers
- Direct mail
- E-mail broadcast
- Fax broadcast
- Media — press release, interviews
- Website (new or existing)
- Free event listings (newspaper, radio)

It's important to get your message out there early, no matter which marketing tools you choose. People need time to think about the event, check their calendars, and plan travel. Try a number of different marketing techniques so your potential audience hears about your event several times. Although you may want to cut costs and work directly with your client in developing all the event marketing materials, you should consider hiring the services of an advertising agency or consultant. You will often see great results from hiring professionals, which provides you with a great return on your investment. Often clients will organize their own advertising and marketing. See chapter 8 for more information on marketing and promotion.

Suppliers

To pull off any meeting or event, you will work with a number of different suppliers, depending on your needs. The next chapter offers good advice for dealing with suppliers and vendors. Here are just some of the services you might need to solicit from suppliers for a given event:

- Entertainment
- Décor
- Food and beverage
- Audiovisual
- Writing and design
- Photography
- Transportation
- Accommodation

Advice worth remembering: maintain good relations with your suppliers — their role is to make your event successful. Over time, you will develop close relationships with your suppliers that deliver solid benefits to both your businesses. See chapter 14 for detailed information on working with suppliers.

Insurance and Permits

Make sure that you secure the necessary insurance and permits for your event. The requirements will vary from city to city and will depend on the type of activities that are taking place. You should check with your local city hall to find out what if any permits will be required and the associated fees and applicable processes and deadlines. The venue may provide for limited liability and property damages through its own insurance coverage. However, you should secure insurance for these possible outcomes if they are not covered by the venue or the client and seek out what other protections are required. Protecting your company against the worst-case scenario is always worth the extra cost, versus taking the risk and suffering any legal and financial consequences. Seek the advice of a professional insurance agent to find out your options.

Contingency Planning

The most common error in planning events is to assume that nothing will go wrong. Recognizing that mistakes happen is critical in getting to a stage where when things *do* go wrong, you can manage them without causing delay or damage to your event. A contingency plan thoroughly identifies potential issues and problems and methods for addressing each.

As a new special events business, you won't have the firsthand experience to know what to avoid. However, there are ways to predict where problems can occur. By examining the list of expenses in the event budget, you can usually pinpoint some activities that are risky. Ensure that your printed materials, signage, and so on are ordered well in advance of your event date. Include in your action plans reminders to phone and check on the status of your orders. Also ask your suppliers what they would do in the case of something going wrong with your order. Get their answer in writing, whenever possible.

Another aspect of contingency planning is crisis management. This process identifies the potential crises that could take place during an event and defines methods for dealing with each. Rain is not a crisis; rather, it is a problem and requires a contingency plan to be in place. An earthquake is a crisis; so is a fire. Although no one wants to anticipate a crisis, there should be a plan in place that ensures people's safety in the event that one occurs. A terrorist attack during a meeting of high-ranking officials would be a crisis, and it too should be planned for in advance by ensuring that appropriate security measures are in place.

Crisis management planning is today considered by many to be an essential part of any planning process. In the special events business, it varies depending on the type of event being organized. For example, if you are planning a wedding, the potential crises will be much less intimidating than if you are providing event management at a G8 summit where the leaders of the world's most industrialized nations gather. Nevertheless, both situations could be hit by disaster — such as an earthquake, fire, or flood. A crisis is not necessarily a disaster of such magnitude, but it can be extremely damaging to your event and your business if you do not prepare yourself in advance.

It is important for you as a new special events business to consider the ramifications of a problem, disaster, or crisis in every event you plan. Very good resources exist that can introduce you to the thinking behind crisis management, which will, in turn, prepare you for the unexpected. An excellent place to start is online at <www.crisisexperts.com>, the website of the Institute for Crisis Management.

After being in business for years, both of us feel that the best piece of advice we can offer for dealing with emergency situations, whether they are true disasters or just minor annoyances, is to stay calm. Many people, in the face of a crisis, are susceptible to panic; some, it would seem, even thrive on it! Don't be one of them. Make sure your plan identifies a leader for every item on the event agenda, so that those working at the event as well as those attending are assured that all is under control. Staying calm will help you deal with any situation in a logical, effective manner and will showcase you as the professional that you are.

Follow-up

Just because your event or meeting is over doesn't mean your work is over. There is the invoice to send, the bills to pay, and the thank-you letters to write. The latter include thank-you letters to facility staff, who are generally very helpful. Arrange to meet with your client for input from their perspective on how the event unfolded. Your client may want a final written report outlining the event, expenses, revenues, etc., and may specify the exact information to be included. If this has not been specified, you should document for your and your client's benefit the history of the event, especially if the event or one like it is to be held again. For example, a conference report should include the following elements:

- Client's name
- Contact name, phone, and address
- Event name and dates
- Venue name and type (i.e., hotel room, ballroom, meeting rooms, receptions, etc.)
- Budget and any overages
- Logistics and flow of the event
- Attendance (planned and actual)
- Menu (meal schedule and number of attendees)
- Bar and beverage (same as above)
- Office or business equipment
- Room setup (square footage and table setup)
- Audiovisual elements
- Décor and staging
- Breakout sessions
- Entertainment

- Speakers

- vips and/or celebrities

- Hotel rooms booked (types, costs, percentage of the initial room block, booking dates, and number of staff and complimentary rooms)

- Travel used

- Registration (early bird, regular, and on-site)

- Suppliers

- Volunteer

- Staff

- Any evaluation used

Large events benefit from a formal follow-up with one or more post-event meetings. There may be a request to have each event committee member or subcommittee compile a separate report on the task they oversaw and any problems experienced. These comments can then be summarized in a final report to the client. Be sure you keep a copy for yourself!

Finally, do your own evaluation of the event. Write down what went well and what you would do differently next time. Even long-time event planning professionals find ways to improve with each event.

14
Working with Suppliers

No matter how good you become at planning special events, you will always need the help of qualified suppliers and vendors to deliver on the objectives. These are people who can easily make or break your budget or the quality of your event. It is in your best interest as a special events company to establish sound contacts in the world of suppliers and vendors, and to maintain positive working relations. This chapter will help you learn how to find good suppliers, negotiate for the best prices, and ensure you get the supplies and services you want when you want them. In addition, this chapter provides tips on working with the suppliers and vendors you will require most often.

Finding Suppliers and Vendors

Which specific suppliers and vendors you will work with depends quite a bit on the types of events you are planning. Here are the types of suppliers and vendors a special events business may require from event to event, in no particular order.

- Food and beverage
- Transportation
- Accommodation
- Recreation

- Travel agents
- Speaker services
- Security firms
- Décor and design

- Printers
- Party supplies
- Tent rentals
- Photographers
- Registration
- Translation and interpretation
- Signage

- Entertainment
- Audiovisual
- Florists
- Name badges (available from stationers)
- Equipment rentals
- Linen rentals
- Moving vans
- Videographers
- Staffing
- Giftware

- Staging

As you can see from this list, your special events business will require plenty of supplies and services in producing events. Some projects will require you to work directly with your client's suppliers, but most of the time, you yourself will need to secure services. Finding suppliers and vendors is fairly simple. Large venues, for example, may either have in-house services or a list of preferred supply and service providers. In some cases, venues will require you to work with their staff, such as catering, as part of the contract.

You can always find suppliers and vendors listed by category in your local Yellow Pages. Additionally, you can browse special events trade magazines to locate suppliers and vendors. See the appendix for a list of industry periodicals. These publications will include directories plus advertisements for a wide range of suppliers and vendors.

Looking to trade magazines and the Yellow Pages is a quick method for finding suppliers when you are just developing your contacts. However, although these are excellent resources, they do not supply testimonials on the level of service or standard of the product the companies provide. For these, you need to ask other related businesses which suppliers they work with and why. Events associations often have a contact list of local and recommended suppliers. They may also have mixer functions where suppliers and planners can network for potential partnerships.

As you become more immersed in the special events community, you will find that suppliers start looking for you and not the reverse. Indeed, the busy special events company will find that the cold calls start to increase. When suppliers call, ask for a catalogue or a proposal to be mailed to you. Suppliers are usually happy to do this, but some will want to deliver the proposal or catalogue in person. Tell them you would prefer to meet after reviewing their supplies or services. This allows you to avoid a high-pressure situation and lets you review products and prices at your leisure.

Be sure to say that you will call back by a certain date, once you receive their material. And be sure to do it! Take the supplier or salesperson's name and number and place it in your calendar system with a reminder note to yourself. When the day comes, if you have not yet received the material, you can call and let them know. If you have, take the time to review it and then make your return call. If the costs are too high, tell them. Companies are often very flexible and will offer you a better deal to secure your business. The next section provides further details on negotiating with suppliers to get you and your client competitive rates on supplies and services.

Negotiating with Suppliers

Negotiating with suppliers can be a bit overwhelming when you are just starting out in the special events business. It may seem that they have the upper hand because you are new to the industry. Remember, it is your business they want, and they will be trying to please you. But they also have a business to run and they want to make a profit. Therefore, it is the salesperson's job to try to balance getting the business for the long haul with making a good profit in the short term.

As a new special events business, you have a reputation to build and manage as well. You need to establish a good rapport and fair business practices with your suppliers and vendors. Price should not always be your main criterion, just as it won't be when companies hire you. Reliability is not negotiable; quality and price are. Therefore, what you want more than anything is the service. You want to develop a mutually beneficial relationship — this way you both know you can depend on the other in a pinch and that each of you has the other's best interest in mind. This type of symbiotic relationship should be what you strive for. If you are always trying to drive down prices or ask for too much, you will find the best suppliers and vendors will stop doing business with you.

Much of the negotiation depends as much on the type of supplies or services as it does on the suppliers and vendors. Here are some basic considerations to have at hand when you begin sourcing the services and suppliers for your event.

- Get a written quote from at least three sources to compare basic pricing.

- Have a general idea of the costs before you call. (Do some investigating on the internet or ask other businesses.)

- Ask about any extra costs (e.g., shipping, courier charges, packaging, gratuities, service charges).

- Find out about any available discounts (e.g., volume, off-season).

- If applicable, ask how they ensure security, confidentiality, and insurance.

- Ask about product/service specifications (grade and quality).

- Define any timing considerations (yours and theirs).

- Ask about billing, payment schedules, and deposits.

- Discuss delivery and/or setup methods and timing.

- Find out about cancellation and/or attrition policies.

- Investigate client references to find out about problems or concerns and how they were resolved.

- Make sure you know the supplier's history (years in business or financial situation). You don't want to deal with a supplier on the verge of bankruptcy or receivership. Call your local Better Business Bureau or visit <www.bbb.org> for listings in the United States and Canada.

Those are the basics when it comes to calling your suppliers and vendors. Be specific about when you need the service or the supplies. You will want to keep in touch with your suppliers throughout the planning stage. This will help you keep on top of any delays and enable you to discuss methods for resolving the situation if a problem develops.

Tips for Dealing with Regular Suppliers

The previous section gave a general introduction to dealing with all types of suppliers and vendors. Over time, you will develop your own successful methods for securing great supplier relations. We're confident of that. To help you out even more, this section provides detailed tips on dealing with the specific vendors and suppliers most commonly required in the special events industry. For instance, regardless of what type of event you are producing, you will need a venue in which to hold the event. That's why this section begins with venue negotiations.

The venue

By this time, you know what your needs are for a venue. You have identified the number and preferred style and tastes of participants. You will know the event objectives and have identified special considerations for your event, such as wheelchair access, VIP protocols, food and beverage, staffing, room setup and equipment, freight and receiving access and availability, business center access, and any technological requirements for audiovisual components, the media, etc. Your next step is to do the site inspections of hotels and banquet halls. Call ahead and speak to someone in sales or catering. Be as precise about your needs as possible. Ideally, your contact will be very knowledgeable on how to meet your needs. You will want to be open, courteous, and professional, and you should expect as much from your contact. When you find the right venue for your event needs and have worked out the services you will use, get the details down in a written contract.

Hotel accommodations

Most hotels that have meeting and banquet facilities provide accommodations at less than regular rates. If you are planning an event that has been held in the hotel before, the sales manager will be familiar with how accommodation was handled in the past, making it easier for you. Otherwise, you will need to discuss how many hotel guests are expected. For larger events, rooms are booked in blocks. Find out what block sizes are available as well as room rates, types, locations, and whether the hotel offers complimentary rooms or suites for the event organizers and VIPs.

You will also want to find out how the hotel handles no-shows and cancellations. Ask about add-ons such as bellhop and/or concierge services, turndown services, newspaper service, and welcome gifts. Finally, negotiate booking deadlines, deposits, and payment schedules. Prepare for these negotiations by bringing along as much information about your event as you can. Especially in peak season, hotels can be very reluctant to reserve a large block of rooms without the guarantee that they will be filled, and you don't want to wind up paying for vacant rooms. Be conservative and realistic in your requests. And make sure you get the deal in writing!

Food and beverage

People will always remember an event that had great food. Unfortunately, the same can be said about events with bad food. The best way to find a good caterer is to ask friends and other businesses for the names of caterers they would recommend. Similarly, if you have been to an event and you recall the food being really good, call either the venue or, if possible, the organizer of the event and ask for that caterer's name and number. Here are some things to keep in mind when you call a caterer.

- Prices will vary, so get at least three caterers to prepare a menu and budget for your event.

- Ask about availability for your specific event and ask for a list of references.

- Ask if you can visit their premises to see — and taste — a menu firsthand.

- Ask to see photographs from previous events, so you can get a sense of how artistic and practical their presentation is.

- See if they provide linens, dinnerware or china, and flatware or silver.

- Ask about extra staffing and ensure you know their manner of dress, as this can be important when you are working on a black tie or formal event.

Additional negotiations with food and beverage companies can include beverage and bar service, table centerpieces, decorations, and party favors. In your final negotiations, you need to discuss taxes, gratuities, deposits, and payment schedules. As always, get all the agreed-upon details in a written contract. Stay in touch with the caterer in the pre-event stages. Always check in with them a week before and the day before to ensure you know exactly when they will arrive.

Printing and signage

The main consideration with printing and signage is not to leave them to the last minute. Indeed, handling these details should be among your first priorities, because both processes take time. The negotiations you undertake with signage and printing companies do not vary much from those of other suppliers and vendors. Ask for references, and discuss timing, cost-cutting opportunities, quality and quantity, shipping and courier costs, and taxes and billing. Depending on the size of the job you need, you should allow two to four weeks for the production, not delivery, of your products. It is possible for smaller jobs to take as little as three days, but in many cases, rush charges will apply. And in smaller communities, printers may not be available, adding time to the schedule. In terms of prices, you will find that the simpler your request, the lower the price. The more creative you get, the higher the cost. If you have a tight budget, keep color and graphics to a minimum and ask about different types of materials for both your printing and signage needs.

Audiovisual

The range of services provided by audiovisual companies is growing as fast as the technology they supply is developing. Many corporations these days want to feature multimedia presentations at their events and sound and light during their banquet functions. Talk to your client and develop a wish list. You can then source the costs and get back to your client to determine whether the desire to go all out is worth the expense in terms of meeting the event's overall objectives.

You will need to be precise about your needs in order for audiovisual negotiations to proceed smoothly. For example, if you are managing a press conference, you will want the audiovisual company to provide a microphone, feeds, and a lectern, but will also want someone there to provide staging and hookups and stay on site to troubleshoot if necessary. Decide if you need wireless microphones and sound systems. Additional services may include intercom and translation services, video messaging, and webcasting. You may also want to inquire about special scrims and screens for lighting effects. Tell the company what your needs are and ask about any prepackaged deals and any complimentary equipment. Make sure you know what your venue will provide in terms of in-house technical support and accessibility and how you can coordinate the services.

Photography

Every special events business will need the services of a good photographer. The methods for finding one are the same as for other suppliers — get referrals when possible. But with or without a referral, you will need to meet with the photographer to see samples of their work. If you are dealing with a photography business, make sure you can get the same photographer whose samples you have seen.

Photographers, even commercial ones, are professional artists, and many will try to impose their own ideas on your event. Certainly you will want their artistic and creative input, but the final product needs to meet your and your client's objectives. Ask a lot of questions to get a feel for how the photographer approaches his or her work. You want someone who is professional enough to know what to do, but at the same time will not bristle at every request you make. You want your event to run smoothly, and it won't help if you have a less than cooperative photographer. Make sure you are comfortable with the one you choose. Ideally, you want to find a skilled photographer who has a way of putting people at ease. This will greatly enhance the end product.

Costs associated with photography will be labor, film, and processing. Make sure you know how long your photographer will spend at your event. Ensure that you know what is considered standard time and what is overtime. Discuss how many photographs you want and whether you want these posed or natural. It is important that you provide the photographer with an event schedule and a shoot list that itemizes the photographs you want (e.g., pre-event, staff, guest speakers, entertainment, etc.). The more details you provide, the more satisfied you will be.

For professional-quality photography, you should be able to look over a contact sheet either by yourself, if the photos are for your own documentary purposes, or with your client, in the case of, say, a wedding. Some photographers will let you keep the contact sheet and order other photos later. Today, many photographers will provide you with the photographs on CD-ROM or send them in an electronic file to an e-mail account or FTP site, which can be very handy for sending images to others, posting them to websites, or including them in documentation later on. Discuss the photographer's manner of processing, any special finishing available (such as glossy or matte) as well as sizing up front. These can affect the costs and will change the look of the finished product. Finally, you will want to discuss processing times, pickup or delivery, and billing.

Entertainment

Many events will require you to book entertainment. Of course, the type of entertainment will depend on the event itself. As a full-service special events business, you should line up a variety of entertainers to offer to your clients. These may include music and live bands, dancers, emcees, comedians, celebrities, speakers, and VIPs. Considerations for sourcing these vendors will be price and type. This section provides a snapshot of some types of entertainment you may require.

Children's parties

When thinking about entertainment for children's parties, develop themes and go from there. The usual vendors and suppliers include clowns, magicians, comedians, artists, balloon sculptors, face painters, cartoon or movie characters, costume suppliers (think glamor girls, princesses, pirates, cowboys, and villains), pony rides, and inflatable jumpers. There are some very good resources online to help get your creative juices flowing and to find suppliers in your area. Try this Australian website, <www.childrensparties.com.au>, and the Complete Children's Party Survival Guide, <www.kidspartysurvival guide.com>, for some ideas to start.

Live and canned music

With regard to music, make sure your vendor fits in with your theme, then find out the cost. For example, if you are planning a conference in the West that will be attended mostly by officials and dignitaries from out of province or state, consider a Western theme. Hire a country band to play. Often a band that is just starting out or works on a casual basis will ask for a simple honorarium to get the exposure your event will provide.

We recommend using the services of an entertainment agency that specializes in booking entertainment. If your city doesn't offer such a service, another good method for finding bands or musical talent is to contact local entertainment venues, such as music halls, nightclubs, piano bars, and restaurants, that feature live music. Radio stations and college and university music programs will also be able to suggest local or nearby talent for hire.

When you make contact with a music vendor, arrange to get a tape or CD-ROM and ask when they will next do a live performance so you can judge their talent and stage performance yourself. You will want your client's help in making the decision. Ask for references, as you want your musicians to be both reliable and entertaining.

DJs and canned music will be listed in your local Yellow Pages. Ask around for a good supplier, and see what type of music they supply. Discuss availability, rates, and hours of work. Always make sure you understand and can provide any special requirements the entertainers have. This means discussing with them in advance their needs in terms of setup, parking, audiovisual support, dressing rooms, stage size, refreshments, and other services. If you have worked with the venue before, a simple confirmation will be all that is required to ensure their needs can be accommodated; otherwise, a site inspection will be necessary.

Official guests, speakers, and celebrities

Dealing with official guests, VIPs, speakers, and celebrities requires some special considerations, not the least of which is travel and accommodation. Make sure you have secured arrangements prior to calling VIPs, so that these can be offered up front. You should investigate the need for special security provisions and discuss other additional activities or services that might be of interest to your VIPs, celebrities, and their guests. You will want to ensure that you follow appropriate protocols and provide exemplary service.

Official guests

In almost all cases, you will not deal directly with dignitaries and officials; you will deal with their staff. These individuals can fully prepare you for any special protocols including formal names of address, such as Your Honor, Your Worship, and so on. You should also inquire, when appropriate, about any cultural practices or protocols, plus whether there is an appropriate distance that you and others must keep, any particular order of address, and any additional securities or special attendees required. Ensure you pay close attention and that all event staff, volunteers, speakers, and entertainers are aware and agree to follow any formalities required. Gift protocol for VIPs can be quite fun and enlightening, especially for dignitaries from other countries or cultures. Make sure you do your homework so you don't offend your VIP.

Speakers

When possible, ask the client for a list of possible speakers or subject-matter experts, if there are specific topics of focus. If you don't get any help from your client, you can source possibilities through a speakers bureau. Try the American Speakers Bureau, <www.speakersbureau.com>, the National Speakers Association, <www.nsaspeaker.org>, or Speakers' Spotlight, <www.speakers.ca>.

You want to ensure that the speaker and subject matter are appropriate and contribute to the success of the event. When you develop your list of speakers, call and ask for availability and any costs or honorariums expected. Discuss the need for any special equipment or access. If you are publishing information on the speakers on a website or in a program, ask for a synopsis of the speech in time for it to be included. Be sure to thank your speakers personally and formally via a letter sent shortly after the event. You may want to secure the same speaker for another engagement, and treating him or her well will give you a much better chance at doing so.

Celebrities

The use of celebrities when hosting special events is gaining popularity. In particular, having celebrities in attendance is a popular method for ensuring sellout attendance at fund-raisers. If you plan to hire a celebrity, make sure your budget will allow it. Celebrity bookings can cost thousands of dollars for a simple appearance, without any entertainment provided. You will need to locate the celebrity's agent, publicist, publisher, production company, professional association, team, etc., depending on the public figure you are trying to reach. You can also contact an entertainment agency or speakers bureau to find a celebrity for your event.

Keep in mind that celebrities are another form of VIP, and that they will have very special requirements that must be met in order to ensure a satisfactory appearance at your event. If your event includes an auction, you should ask the celebrity to consider donating a personal item, as these tend to receive high bids. Do provide gifts for your celebrities. You will be surprised how many local businesses will be happy to provide you with gifts, so long as their business name is on the product.

Keeping Suppliers and Vendors Happy

As your special events business grows, you will gain more and more contacts in the world of suppliers and vendors. You will gain confidence in your negotiations, and you will likely find that some of your favorite conversations take place with your suppliers. Issues and problems will arise, so don't expect every deal to work out the way you wanted. Be patient and work with each supplier to find a solution that works for you, the supplier, and your client. On event day, remember to treat your suppliers with as much respect as you treat your client and the event participants. Making them happy will really contribute to producing a successful event. Go the extra distance for your favorite suppliers by sending thank-you letters or cards on birthdays and anniversaries, and offer congratulations if your supplier is celebrating a special accomplishment. You will find the return on investment is well worth the effort.

15
The RFP: Getting the Business

There are few things that a business owner enjoys less than preparing a response to a request for proposals, or RFP. However, this is one of the best methods for securing long-range, high-dollar-value projects. Today many government agencies, and some corporate organizations as well, are required to issue an RFP for all contracts over a certain dollar value. The RFP process is aimed at providing the taxpayers or shareholders with the satisfaction that the contract went to the company most qualified, at the best cost. It is also meant to provide the public with the assurance that all eligible and interested companies were given a fair opportunity to secure the project by competing in an open bidding process. The special events business that wants to succeed in winning an RFP would be wise to follow the advice set out in this chapter.

Defining the Bidding Process

Through advertising, word-of-mouth, as well as other sources of marketing and sales, your special events business will create interest and eventually get contracts. However, you can't expect all your business to come through these efforts. On many occasions, even when business comes knocking, you will be called upon to submit a response to an RFP.

There is no one standard format for an RFP. In fact, there are several types of bidding opportunities that a business can respond to. Here are the three most common.

Invitation to quote (ITQ)

An invitation to quote is a less formal process than an RFP, due to a smaller budget for the scope of services required. An ITQ might be used to seek bids from companies on projects with budgets of less than $25,000. Sometimes this process is known as a request for quotations.

Request for proposals (RFP)

A request for proposals is an invitation to companies and contractors to submit a proposal that will demonstrate the ability to deliver, in a cost-effective manner, on the objectives of a project. An RFP is typically used by governments and public organizations on projects with budgets of more than $25,000.

Request for qualifications (RFQ)

A request for qualifications is an invitation to companies and contractors to submit a response that demonstrates professional ability and experience in delivering specific services. The hiring company can then pull from the respondents shortlisted through the RFQ process for specific projects. Companies may be directly awarded a contract for a project or subject to an ITQ or bidding process. It should be made clear that there is no guarantee that a company shortlisted will be awarded a contract. (A direct award or "sole sourced" contract is a process that bypasses public bidding. It may be used when there is only one known supplier capable of delivering the services or when unique circumstances, such as confidentiality or timing, make it a necessity.)

Regardless of what the process is, a response to a formal bidding process should not be taken lightly. Once again, you need to do some homework before you consider submitting a response. The next section helps your special events business improve its chances of making it through the detailed process toward winning the contract.

Competing for an RFP

The RFP process is usually very formal and will not allow you much contact with the potential client. There may be a formal orientation session for proponents to attend, at which those competing have an opportunity to ask questions. Alternatively, there may be a contact listed to whom questions must be either faxed or e-mailed. All of these questions are then documented and the responses made available to any and all potential proponents. It is possible that you may be able to speak to one of the decision-makers directly, which provides you with an excellent chance to make a personal impression as well as gain insight into the potential contract and the client's goals and objectives. Again, it really depends on the client.

The formalization of the process is aimed at keeping it open and transparent so that no special treatment occurs to compromise the competition. As a new special events business, do not be put off by this process. Even if your business does not get shortlisted in the initial phase, responding to an RFP is good experience. Your company will be provided with feedback. Make sure you get detailed information about your company's strengths and weaknesses in comparison to the other proponents.

As mentioned, the less formal RFP process may allow you to meet with the client to discuss the RFP in detail prior to submitting it. Having the perfect qualifications will not make a difference unless you are clear on the client's expectations — this is a vital part of winning the contract. Where possible, find out if there is an incumbent or special events company currently providing services to the client. There will be times that an RFP process is predetermined. Although this can be off-putting to a potential proponent, even these occasions can be good for business. It's not likely a client will tell you they know whom they are choosing, unless you have an inside contact. Therefore, you may be exposed to rumors and speculation. Submitting a response will still provide your special events business with an opportunity to be seen as a future consideration, should anything change with respect to the "chosen" events service provider or the amount of work the client needs.

The Basics of an RFP

Competing in an RFP process is time-consuming, but you can become expert at it by just following the rules. RFPs will vary in relation to the potential business. The time and cost your company will be asked to invest should be in direct relation to the complexity and cost of a potential contract. It is unlikely that you will be asked to respond to a 50-page RFP for a potential contract valued at less than $10,000. Nor is it likely that you will be able to send in a simple letter to compete for a one-year contract with a budget of $125,000. Regardless of the size of the potential contract, all RFPS have common elements. The RFP will outline key contacts, desired and mandatory criteria, response process and any presentations or portfolio materials that must be supplied, and the time line. An RFP might include the following specifics:

(a) Background on the client

(b) Outline of the budget (not always provided)

(c) Purpose of the event

(d) Scope of the work

(e) Target audience

(f) Date of event or time frame for services

(g) Goals and objectives

(h) Types of events planned

(i) Stakeholders (others involved both internal and external to the client)

(j) Roles and responsibilities of the contractor

(k) Scoring criteria

Your response strategy will require extensive research and attention to detail. You will want to show creative and strategic ability. Your response must cover all the subject matter requested, both mandatory and desired. A qualified special events business can be disqualified from the process by a simple omission of a signature. Be sure to read over the RFP carefully, for you will need to follow instructions line by line. The next section helps guide you through preparing your response.

Preparing Your Response

Once you have had an opportunity to review the RFP in detail and attend an orientation session or ask the contact questions, you are ready to prepare your response. A great way to start your response is by analyzing the structure of the RFP. Develop an outline for your response based on the elements listed. Make notes on each section as to what you need in order to showcase your event skills and abilities in their best light. List the client's goals and objectives and develop a plan that clearly demonstrates how you will meet them. If you do not have direct experience providing the services requested, outline where you do have experience and clearly outline any similarities and transferable skills and abilities.

Your response will need to demonstrate your strategic planning abilities and your approach to the business. Take your time in preparing your response, and try to avoid assuming that the client will understand all that is involved in providing your services. Write your response as though the client had no idea what you do. This way, you will be more likely to provide the adequate amount of detail.

Developing Your Sample Event

You will need to approach the potential project on which you are bidding as you would any project you are assigned. You need to clearly plan the event from start to finish. Follow the processes laid out in chapter 13, starting with an event plan. Without the benefit of discussion, you will need to make some assumptions in your planning. Using the RFP as a template, determine as best you can the goals and objectives of the event and work from there. Be sure to include the rationale for your strategies and the expected outcome. Bring the potential event to life for the RFP evaluators. Develop and describe in detail, as appropriate, your proposed theme, agenda, time line, venue, and budget along with any additional components such as food and beverage services, signage, printing, décor, gifts and takeaways, entertainment, speakers, administration, registration or ticket sales, sponsorships, partners, media, marketing and public relations, transportation, accommodation, recreation, and tourist activities for spouses and guests (or for event participants as time allows), etc. Provide a method for evaluating success and any follow-up activities that you will provide.

Your response will need to show how you can provide extra value to their proposed event or to the client. Show that you will be 100 percent committed to meeting their budget and delivering on time. As well as preparing a sample event, you will likely need to include a case study or example of an event you have worked on and how you were successful in reaching the objectives. Show your methods for measuring success and how these can be applied to this potential contract. You will need to supply references. Where practical, include written references or testimonials from satisfied clients. You may also be asked to submit a statement on confidentiality and conflicts of interest.

Meeting the Budget

Preparing a cost estimate can be difficult, but it can be one of the most critical areas of an RFP process. You need to show how you can work within the client's budget and yet provide a high-quality return on investment.

Provide as much information as possible, and be specific. It is far better to include too much information than too little. Forecast detailed expenses and any potential revenue sources, such as registration fees or ticket sales. You may want to add a section on how your special events business can add value through partnerships and/or sponsorships.

Be careful to follow the required format stated in the RFP, and lay out any expenses in the most comprehensive manner you can. Indicate that these are by no means exhaustive, and that you fully expect that the details of expenses will develop with more information on the client's goals. Use the checklist provided in chapter 13 to help you identify potential costs, both fixed and variable. You may also be asked to break down administrative costs by service, such as management fees, on-site registration fees, strategic planning fees, etc. Whatever method you choose, a flat rate, blended rate, hourly wage, or daily rate, be sure to indicate that you are willing to negotiate your terms to ensure that the client's needs are met. Many contracts are awarded on the basis of quality of service, not cost, and offering flexibility is just one more way to show that your special events business is committed to providing the highest level of service possible.

Looks Count: Presentation of Your Response

Trust us on this: looks do count! Most RFP and bidding processes for substantial contract opportunities elicit a good response from competing companies. Imagine that you are on the receiving end of these submissions. Would you be impressed by a sloppy, hard-to-follow response? No, of course you wouldn't, so put some effort into the appearance of your response. The form of presentation need not be expensive, but your submission should be on clean paper, clearly laid out with a cover letter, table of contents, executive summary, client list, case studies, budget, time line, and fees.

Although there is no need to get elaborate with colored or odd-sized paper, you could look into preparing your own response template with added features such as using a watermark for a thematic design element or embossing the paper for textural polish. You should also consider the method of binding you use. Stapling is the standard method, but other options for smaller documents should be considered, such as a spiral or coil binding, which allow a document to lay flat when opened. Saddle-stitching — which uses staples in the center of a document — is also commonly used for binding smaller documents.

You may want to develop a cover for your proposal that attracts attention and can be developed to represent either your special events business brand or the theme of the event you are bidding on. Discuss options with your designer and printer when you are ready to take your proposals to the next step. The costs can run high, but the payoffs can be great. If you want to be taken as a professional and compete against well-established special events businesses, you'll want to look the part.

However you approach the look and feel of your response, do not overlook the basic requirements. Make sure your proposal package is sent on time to the right contact, contains the appropriate number of copies, and has the RFP title, closing time, and address clearly visible.

Presenting with Polish

Most RFP processes will include an oral component. This is where you will be expected to provide details on your written proposal in person in front of a panel. The panel members may or may not have seen your written proposal. Do not assume that this element of the process is scored along with the written proposal. It may be judged on its own merit and require the details to be as comprehensive as those included in the written submission.

Most presentations will be about an hour to two hours in length and will be broken down into elements that were covered in your written submission. This is your chance to introduce your approach in living color. If you are not comfortable speaking publicly, rehearse with a few friends first. You will likely be given an outline to follow. Make sure you follow it. Do consider using additional presentation methods that can be developed on your computer using the aid of presentation software; for instance, *Microsoft PowerPoint*.

Always supply a hard copy of your presentation up front, for this saves panel members the burden of taking extensive notes. You can also provide your presentation on CD-ROM. Find out what kind of presentation equipment will be provided and be familiar with hookups and operation of the equipment before you go. Time your presentation well, and be prepared to answer questions. Try not to ramble, and do try to gauge your presentation's success as you go. The expressions and body language of the panel should be your guide; if they look bored, move faster and add energy.

Interviewing can be a dreary process for your panel members. As a special events professional, you should be engaging and very aware of the time, but you must also be yourself. There is no point in trying to adopt a new persona strictly for the sake of a presentation. Try to be comfortable and in control. Speak clearly and with conviction, and answer any questions in a polite and thorough manner. Do not speak to one panel member; engage all panel members and address them by name as much as possible. Be diplomatic and keep jokes to a minimum. Panel members do not want to waste their time with those who do not take their time seriously.

As part of your presentation, you should be prepared to show samples of your work. See chapter 12 for some pointers on developing a professional portfolio to showcase your work.

Following Up

As it is with any competition, you can't win them all. Do not get discouraged; the selection process is very difficult and often the most qualified companies do not come first. The variables are great, and the specifics of each competition will dictate the winner of the award. The best you can do is learn from the competitive process you enter by asking for a full debriefing of how you fared in each segment of the competition and how you measured against the competitors overall. Once you have had your debriefing session, send a thank-you note to your contact for his or her time and consideration, and ask for a call the next time a contract goes up for bid and a referral to other potential clients. Take it from us — this is a nice touch and one that is likely to be remembered.

16
Award-Winning Events

The special events business is always one of creativity, ingenuity, and hard work. While you may work on many events for which it seems the client's wishes require far more of your perspiration than inspiration, you will also have plenty of opportunity to mine your own creative depths. It may be that you have already attended a memorable event or two for which the organizers went beyond the ordinary and created an experience never to be forgotten. An event like that may even have sparked your interest in the field itself. It isn't easy to carry off an extraordinary event. For that reason, the organizers of such events (and in some cases, the clients) often enter them into award contests.

With this in mind, we approached the organizers of six award-winning events and included descriptions of those events here, in the organizers words, to help inspire and entertain you. In recognition of the diversity of the events and their producers, we have left the write-ups as close to their original submissions as word count would permit. Read through the following pages and see for yourself how each of the producers went about planning, executing, and then summarizing his or her event. The challenges were as different for each event as the write-ups themselves, but what remains the same throughout each extraordinary event is the degree of dedication, imagination, and attention to detail, as well as the passion of the producers to push the boundaries of this fascinating and constantly evolving field.

It would not be wise to tackle events on the scale of the six described below while you are still feeling your way around the business. The quality of these events is, however, something to strive for. We are confident that within a few years, your events, too, will be winning awards, and you will be creating events that will remain in the minds of the lucky event participants and inspire the next generation of special events businesses!

These are the events described in this chapter:

- **Fashion Cares 2003 — Viva Glam Casino:** 2004 Canadian Event Industry Awards

- *John "Q" Movie Premiere:* 2003 ISES Esprit Award/2003 *Special Events Magazine*'s Gala Awards

- **Cirque Pacifique:** 2004 Canadian Event Industry Awards

- **Malavalli/Patel Wedding:** 2004 Canadian Event Industry Awards

- **Christmas through the Eyes of a Child**: 2004 Canadian Event Industry Awards

- **Last Tango in Paris:** 2004 *Special Events Magazine*'s Gala Awards

Fashion Cares 2003 — Viva Glam Casino

Event Management Company/Producer: Eatertainment Special Events and the Fashion Cares Steering Committee

Website: www.eatertainment.com/www.fashioncares.com

Category of Entry/Name of Award (#1): Best Event Produced for a Charitable Organization, 2004 Canadian Event Industry Awards

Category of Entry/Name of Award (#2): Event of the Year, 2004 Canadian Event Industry Awards

Date of Event: May 31, 2003

Location of Event: Toronto, Canada

Name of Client: ACT (Aids Committee of Toronto)

Fashion Cares 2003 brought together 6,000 guests for the sole purpose of celebrating the conviction that one day a cure will be found for AIDS and events such as this one will no longer be needed.

In the meantime, however, and for the past 17 years, it has been the task of the Fashion Cares Steering Committee to raise money through the Fashion Cares Gala for the Aids Committee of Toronto. The Fashion Cares Gala is the single-largest fundraising event in benefit of ACT. Each year, hundreds of volunteers spend the better part of a year working to produce the gala.

Fashion Cares begins at 5:30 p.m. with a gala patron reception and ends nearly 12 hours later when the last guests leave the after party. The event includes dinner for 3,000, a fashion show featuring more than 60 Canadian designers and world-renown performers, a silent auction and boutique that generate more than $100,000 in revenue, and an after-party for 6,000 that lasts into the wee hours of the morning. This year's event transported guests into the era of vintage casino and raised more than $750,000 for ACT.

The challenges we faced included the following:

- Developing a theme consistent with the Fashion Cares mantra of "more than an event"

- Securing sponsors to subsidize a large portion of the evening's expenses

- Developing a cocktail-party concept for 4,500 guests and securing donated canapés to feed these guests

- Planning, designing, and producing a formal dining room — casino themed — and ensuring the smooth execution of dinner for 3,000

- Planning, designing, and producing a boutique, casino, and the silent-auction portion of the evening with more than 30 featured retailers

- Securing top-tier talent to headline the fashion show and concert

- Planning and producing a fashion show and concert for roughly 4,500 guests, which featured Canadian fashions and world-renown entertainment, once again with the objective of wowing the audience

- Planning, designing, and managing a lounge for VIP guests

- Planning, designing and producing an after-party for approximately 6,000 guests

- Securing media exposure before, during, and after the event to ensure the success of this year's event and future events

- Ensuring the event did not exceed its budget expenses

- Ensuring that each area of this multi-faceted event ran smoothly

Each challenge was met with enthusiasm and was overcome in the following ways.

Theme

Philip Ing, the creative director of Fashion Cares, chose the theme of casino. His vision of Rat Pack meets *Ocean's Eleven* embodied the opulence and eccentricity of vintage Sin City. This vision was carried throughout all seven parts of the event. As guests made their way from room to room, the theme flowed evenly.

No one previously had done a casino theme on the scale or grandeur of the Fashion Cares Casino.

Sponsorship

The sponsorship team succeeded in securing title sponsors for all key areas of the event, each a returning sponsor from the previous year. Additionally, more than 12 national and local media sponsors were secured, along with dozens of financial sponsors and hundreds of sponsors-in-kind, ranging from retailers to caterers, to private individuals.

Cocktail reception

Guests were treated to a cocktail reception hosted by Iceberg Vodka, with more than 14,000 donated canapés from almost a dozen of Toronto's top caterers. With hanging sheers and lucite panels, the cocktail area was dazzling for the 4,500 guests who attended. Specialty martinis and champagne were some of the featured beverages, alongside traditional wines, beers, and full bar rail.

Dining room

Dinner for 3,000 was set to the theme of vintage casino elegance. The dining room was scattered with lit tables in the title sponsor's colors of yellow, red, green, and blue. The tables were decorated with ice centerpieces that were carved as playing cards, lit from beneath, and which had the Fashion Cares branding within them. The menu was based on traditional elegant dining, starting with a shrimp cocktail served from an ice bowl, followed by Calvados-infused chicken stuffed with a julienne of wild mushroom and country apple, and accompanied by diamond- and heart-shaped Yukon Gold potato towers. Guests commented that the dinner was excellent, and far more memorable than any previous year.

Boutique, silent auction, casino

The boutique was executed with the participation of more than 30 prominent retailers. The silent auction comprised more than 150 items, including works of art from prominent Canadian artists. The casino hosted guests throughout the evening as they tried their luck at the tables. Theses three areas were seamlessly integrated to form a retail component that made a significant contribution to the evening's revenues.

Talent

Through the hard work of the committee, and with a bit of luck, Fashion Cares 2003 was able to secure world-class talent, featuring Sarah Brightman performing songs from her newly released album, *Harem*, and Chantal Kreviazuk performing the richly arranged piano ballads that have made her a multi-platinum selling artist. Jully Black and Matt Dusk also performed.

Fashion show

Philip Ing brought to this year's event more than 60 Canadian designers, each creating custom pieces matching the theme of casino. The culmination of the show was the unveiling of the Mac Viva Glam "House of Cards," a series of body-paint designs by renowned artists and celebrities. Twenty completely nude models walked the catwalk to end the show and begin the after-party.

VIP Lounge

The VIP lounge was designed to bring the exclusive club look to Fashion Cares, and offer gala patrons an alternative to the after-party. Hosted by DJ Chaba Khan, the VIP lounge provided an elegant but modern setting for guests to enjoy while they sipped fine Mumm's champagne.

After-party

The line-up of talent for the after-party was one of the best ever. Performers included Hex Hector, DJ Matt C, Widelife, and Lena Love (a seven-foot-tall drag queen). Guests danced until past 5 a.m. — a sure sign the evening was a success.

Media

Media coverage was excellent. Circulation/audience reached by category was as follows:

Print: 16,507,366

Radio: 930,000

Television: 9,642,000

Budget

The event expenses came in at 5 percent below budget, and 12 percent below the previous year's expenses — a huge success.

Co-ordination

The event began on time, stayed on schedule, and was in every aspect a huge success. Moving guests from the reception to the dining room, then to the fashion show, and finally to the after-party was no small task, but was executed flawlessly.

In a year ravaged by SARS, blackouts, and much more, we were able to control costs, maintain ticket sales, and make the event an amazing evening for all in attendance.

John "Q" Movie Premiere

Event Management Company/Producer: An Original Occasion

Website: www.aooevents.com

Category of Entry/Name of Award (#1): Event Design Budget $0.00 – $50,000.00, 2003 ISES Esprit Award

Category of Entry/Name of Award (#2): Best Theme Décor with a Total Décor Budget $20,000.00 – $50,000.00, 2003 *Special Events Magazine*'s Gala Awards

Date of Event: February 7, 2002

Location of Event: Director's Guild of America, Los Angeles, California

Name of Client: New Line Cinema

This Hollywood film premiere went from client phone call to reality *within nine working days*. After reviewing the movie and promotional material, it was easy for us to capture the color scheme for the event, but the theme was more difficult! The film took place in a hospital emergency room that was held captive by a man whose child was dying. What a theme!

We decided to capture the feel of the movie in the décor for the premiere. By zoning in on the clean, sterile feel of the emergency room, with its chrome tables, white beds, white drapes, and simple, direct lighting, the theme started to come alive. After reviewing the promo material, we added the colors of blue and parchment. The tricky thing was not only that we had to design the event for the high-profile, celebrity-studded audience, but also that we had to design it so that it could be set up during the short time that the movie ran — which meant less than two hours!

A word was never written! No formal proposal was ever presented! There wasn't time! The event was sold by computer drawing alone.

The event's design was tailored to the event purpose. The client desired an event that would not only impress its star-studded Hollywood guest list, but that would also be appealing to the paparazzi waiting outside the doors. The design was entirely custom-built for the premiere's after-party. The design was not the only issue, though; the timing was as well. The event had to be designed for a fast set-up: only one hour and 18 minutes. Every décor element had to be built and designed based on theme as well as on ease of set-up. After hours of placement and set treatment, the items were tagged and the entire event came down, to be re-assembled again only once we had word that all guests had moved into the premier.

When the magic hour struck, so did the crew. The buffet tables were made of galvanized steel façades, hand tooled and finished especially for the event. These popped up around six-foot banquet tables. Faux parchment-colored leather cap linens were custom made and slipped right on the tables. The buffet décor on the four large buffets was made up of 47 chrome lamps with white lampshades — much like the ones in the movie — with custom dyed cobalt blue roses and wheat grass arranged in a ring around the base of each lamp. With all-white china and all-chrome service ware, the look was clean, trendy, and definitely cool.

The bars took on a similar look with matching custom steel fronts and custom white faux leather cap linens; only this time, giant six-foot-diameter all-white lampshades were suspended overhead.

The guests' seating took on a new look with a series of three different styles in cocktail tables. Cap-styled tabletop linens were custom made in special textured fabrics. Each piece of linen was made specially to fit the tables exactly, with a six-inch drop all around. One of the looks used a 36-inch stand-up cocktail table with a single chrome post. A poodle-loop ice-blue fabric was used for the linen cap. A lamp with a baby-blue lampshade and chrome post, with white roses and wheat grass at the base, matched the buffet lamps, but with a twist on the color. The second table design used a white loop-textured fabric cap with blue roses in a cobalt blue vase and matching ice-blue poodle-loop fabric chair covers. The third table was a textured parchment fabric in the same cap-style linen and blue-rose arrangement, but the chairs were steel, matching the bar and buffet façades.

However, cocktail tables weren't the only guest seating to be found. Three eigth-foot by eight-foot daybeds were scattered around the room, every one with sheer white drapes that went floor to ceiling and which were up lit in ice-blue. The beds were covered in a light-parchment and baby-blue damask fabric. The covers had hospital corners, and there was a neatly stacked pile of white and blue pillows in the centers of the daybeds.

Stainless-steel bed trays sat on one corner of the daybeds, and held a small, cobalt blue vase and floral arrangement. Highlighting the daybeds were matching giant lampshades hung over the center of each bed, which served to tie the beds' decor back to the bar décor.

Lighting design was key to this space. The Directors Guild building has one wall of glass, one wall of dark wood, and the rest are white with metal inserts. To deal with the different textures of the walls and tie them all together, they were washed with textured patterns and soft complimentary colors. Scrolling verbiage from the film's website inspired us to subtly introduce the client's logo and movie name into the design by scrolling gobo projections of JOHN Q and the client's logo slowly over the daybeds to the walls, and having these dissolve and reappear. This unobtrusive movement was created by intelligent lighting and programming. The room seemed to evolve constantly as guests moved from buffet to bar, to the tables.

Cirque Pacifique

Event Management Company/Producer: BC Event Management

Website: www.bceventmanagement.com

Category of Entry/Name of Award (#1): Best Entertainment Event Produced for a Corporation, 2004 Canadian Event Industry Awards

Category of Entry/Name of Award (#2): Most Outstanding Event $100,000 – $300,000, 2004 Canadian Event Industry Awards

Date of Event: August 14, 2003

Location of Event: BC Place Stadium, Vancouver, British Columbia

Name of Client: International Conference Services (ICS)

The event was a gala banquet for a prestigious international medical conference, the 10th World Conference on Lung Cancer, in Vancouver, British Columbia. The banquet for 2,000 guests took place in the local football stadium.

BC Event Management (BCEM) was tasked by International Conference Services (ICS) with producing a successful world-class cirque-style production, in a venue totally unsuitable for theater and for rigging (therefore unsuitable for cirque shows). We had to overcome the stark sports lighting and bad stadium acoustics, and also the large audience, which could easily have felt disconnected from the stage.

We met these challenges by assembling a top-tier lineup of performers, overcoming the limitations of the venue, and topping the event off with a world-first finalé performance: a trapeze act suspended under a hot air balloon! Welcome to Cirque Pacifique.

The venue was a stark, cavernous 60,000-seat stadium. Because the Teflon/fabric air-suspended roof of the stadium let in diffuse daylight, we delayed the start of the show until sunset. With this scheduling and through the use of a very high velour drape surround, we were able to control what the guests experienced. We created a warm environment within a vast endless space.

The hot-air balloon hovered behind the stage, creating a colorful backdrop and filling the void of the unused half of the field.

Because the production consisted of assembled individual acts rather than an existing (and, therefore, well-rehearsed) troupe, we worked extremely hard to create the slick production values the guests would anticipate from what they would expect was an established team. The cirque troupe that BCEM had contracted went bankrupt months before the event. Other troupes were no longer available. BCEM had no choice but to create its own human circus. It created Cirque Pacific.

We hired dozens of children from a local circus school to animate the guests' entrance. The kids juggled, unicycled, and performed acrobatics during the guests' arrival.

The evening was scheduled to include multiple performances between the dinner courses. We were concerned about holding the attention of 2,000 guests at table rounds covering 25,000 square feet, but this very international crowd was captivated by every act and was completely attentive. An audience can easily become attention fatigued if they are hit with too much for too long. However, by never competing with food service and by breaking up the acts, we stayed fresh throughout with more than 60 minutes of performances.

To make the guests at the tables at the back of the venue feel included in the activity, we performed four acts from rigging points suspended over these tables. To light these acts, which were far from the stage lighting, we brought in six Super Trouper follow spots and installed them on 20-foot-high scaffold towers.

We masked the scaffold towers with velour drape and integrated them into the perimeter drape runs of the same height. This resulted in the towers "disappearing." The camera risers were placed at back of the huge "room," thereby clearing sightlines. This effect was accomplished by utilizing expensive extra-long camera lenses.

The circus kids promenaded throughout the venue all night, including between stage acts, and tied the whole evening together thematically.

BCEM created a custom bright-orange circular stage to support the cirque theme. (To complement the theme, ICS covered the tables in strong colors and covered the chairs with black chair covers.)

Three of the acts were embellished by stage pyrotechnics.

The venue was seen as a liability because it is so cavernous, but we succeeded in turning this liability into an asset. Supporting this endeavor were the three extremely high routines, which were used to take advantage of the available height in a dramatic fashion. These were —

1) the high (blue and red) silk routines out among the tables,

2) the hot air balloon, and

3) two custom-built "sky ladders" that rose 50 feet in the air to serve as a performance apparatus.

Malavalli/Patel Wedding

Event Management Company/Producer: He Loves Me

Website: www.helovesme.ca

Category of Entry/Name of Award: Best Wedding, 2004 Canadian Event Industry Awards

Date of Event: September 4–6, 2003

Location of Event: Malavalli family home, Toronto, Ontario; Fairmont Royal York Hotel, Toronto, Ontario (wedding reception)

Name of Client: Malavalli family

Our client looked to us to plan, design, and produce the ultimate wedding, which would not only consider the traditions of both Indian families but would also reflect the couple's modern approach to life, love, and happiness.

To achieve this feat, we had first to understand who the bride and groom were, both individually and as a couple. Armed with this information, we then looked at the couple's preliminary thoughts on their wedding and at how to incorporate those individual and couple traits into the design of the wedding.

This approach is how we develop the concept of each event, or, as we like to say, develop the vision. We feel this approach is key to the success of any event, particularly an event as intimate as a wedding.

Typically, once we understand who the couple is, to aid in the development of ideas, we do some external research on the ethnicity of both the bride and the groom. Since we had little knowledge of the Hindu culture and no knowledge of the Gujarat community, this research was beneficial, as it allowed us to respectfully combine these two cultures.

Once we had developed the overall vision and received our client's approval, we then began research into all the elements involved in this project. We needed to decide which aspects we could handle internally and which elements we would need help with, all the while keeping in mind how the client would be happiest.

In the instances in which we decided to outsource, we needed truly to understand each service provider's capabilities. We had to trust them, and we needed the vendors to be comfortable with our authority on the project (we look very young!).

Our first step was to provide each of them with a copy of the vision for the event and ask each of them how he or she would achieve his or her respective objective. Then, taking the proposals that we felt were in line with our objectives, we set up a "meet and greet" with the service providers to further explore their ability to be creative and work as a team. We also asked them for references from suppliers in other categories with whom they had had good experiences. After comparing the recommendations with the proposals — and then checking with our gut — we ended up with an amazing group of individuals who went above and beyond every step of the project!

While this was happening, we also worked on nurturing our relationship with our client(s) and sought their decisions so that the project could move forward. To do this though, we needed to meet with the clients. Unfortunately for us, the bride traveled quite a bit; the groom lived in London, England; and her parents, who were paying for the whole event, lived in California. Indeed, it was a big challenge to keep the project moving along while accommodating everyone's schedule.

Nonetheless, we had created a bang-on vision, found a top-notch group of individuals to help us put it all together — and the event was less than two weeks away. It was time to stop talking and start building.

With more than 45 vendors hired to execute the three days of events, ensuring that everything happened flawlessly and on schedule, and without disruption to the 15 visiting houseguests — while also getting enough sleep to function the next day — was an adventure. We weren't sure we were going to survive!

Fortunately, since we crossed all the Ts and dotted all the Is, it went very smoothly. Even when it didn't, neither the clients nor the guests were privy to anything other than perfection.

Christmas through the Eyes of a Child

Event Management Company/Producer: Decor & More Inc.

Website: www.decorandmore.com

Category of Entry/Name of Award: Best Theme Décor, 2004 Canadian Event Industry Awards

Date of Event: December 2003

Location of Event: Oakville, Ontario

The mandate for this event was a grand one. The objective: create a once-in-a-lifetime, show-stopping event that would transform the room and leave those in attendance in awe. The guests were a sophisticated audience, so we were asked to think creatively and develop concepts that would differ from any they had experienced before. In addition, to enhance the look of the event, we were asked to incorporate numerous forms of motion into the event design, and we were also asked to have several things revealed or made to occur throughout the evening. A last-minute request required us to include an element that would be somewhat interactive and provide a take-home aspect for the attendees.

For just one night, guests were returned to the days of their childhood, when Christmas was the most exciting time of the year and everything seemed larger than life because it was all viewed through the wide-eyed innocence of youth.

As attendees passed through the entrance from the cocktail space to the dining area, the large evergreen archway, which was enhanced with regular-size toys, gave way to a second, surreal experience as the guests passed under the interior archway, which was decorated with outsized toys, candy, and other childhood fantasies.

A pair of spotlights hit two puppeteers peering over the interior entranceway, and the light traveled down the strings to the "human" puppets in very large costumes. These actors on puppet strings welcomed guests to the incredible oversized environment.

Once inside, guests were immersed in a world in which they felt small in comparison to their surroundings. Every aspect was seen from a child's perspective and all were married in a stylized combination of *Honey I Shrunk the Kids* meets *Toy Story*.

The focal point of the room was the show-stopping, growing Christmas tree. This tree, which started at eight feet tall, eventually expanded to a height of 30 feet through the use of a manfrotto system, and its star was lit by a flying angel during the high point of the evening's festivities. An arrangement of very large gifts with lush bows and tags was ensconced at the base of the tree.

The perimeter of the room featured ten displays of outsized toys atop risers, for full viewing impact when guests were dining. Each riser measured 24 feet in length by 12 feet in depth and showcased larger-than-life displays of huge toys, gigantic trinkets, colossal candy, and massive presents — both opened and unopened — for an utterly overpowering environment. Large, impressive, displays were tiered up to the 21-foot-high mark (an 18-foot display atop a 3-foot riser) and a depth of 12 feet in dimensional vignettes, making for high impact and drama under theatrical lighting.

Here, atop the risers, collages of huge, sought-after items were artfully displayed. Playful vignettes of an eight-foot Raggedy Ann and Andy riding a seven-foot rocking horse, and a 12-foot-high, three-dimensional Jack in the Box were showcased along with giant cascading sheet music at 10 feet high and an eight-foot guitar. Some items were peeking out of the oversized gift boxes, and others were totally open amid bows and paper.

Another vignette showcased an eight-foot, larger-than-life, Barbie-style doll, real, still in its collector box with the cellophane front, a large 10-foot rotating music box with a crystal princess, and an outsized toy wagon with huge toy blocks. Still another display had a pair of 12-foot-high massive toy soldiers, large jacks and balls, outsized chess pieces, and a Monopoly board, crayons, paint brushes, and six-foot dominos, as well as oversized sporting equipment.

Ultra-large gifts both wrapped and unwrapped, outsized ornaments, giant gift tags, deliciously massive candy canes, lollipops, and peppermint candies as well as oversized gingerbread cookies and stylized trees were interwoven into all of the vignettes. The ceiling was lowered for intimacy with a swagging treatment of ivory, green, and red gossamer, as well as a few very large four-foot ornaments.

An impressive 28-foot train motored around the space, carrying presents throughout, and pulled up for photo ops in the interior of the room. In addition, operational candy stores allowed guests to indulge in sweet treats to eat on site or take home.

Tables were designed with beautifully textured red linen, and featured a battery-operated turntable showcasing a gingerbread house atop a snow-dusted evergreen base, creating the illusion of a music box. Five votive candles surrounded the pieces, creating instant tabletop illumination. Napkins in red were paired with chair covers in black with red bands, to add depth and drama to the tables. A cellophane-wrapped gingerbread cookie with festive bow was the perfect touch as the napkin treatment.

This wonderful environment allowed guests, if only for one night, to return to the innocence of youth and view the world in the wide-eyed excitement — through the eyes of a child.

Last Tango in Paris

Event Management Company/Producer: A Legendary Event

Website: www.alegendaryevent.com

Category of Entry: Best Wedding Produced For An Individual, 2004 International *Special Events Magazine*'s Gala Awards

Date of Event: May 10, 2003

Location of Event: The Event Loft at Underground, Atlanta, Georgia

Name of Client: Libby Collier and Josh Terrell

Though our bride looked more like the young Parisian actress in the French film *Amélie* than Maria Schneider in *Last Tango in Paris*, this young woman intended to marry with flair and drama. After a long weekend of partying in Amsterdam, the actual wedding ceremony was to be held on the steps of the Sacre Coeur in Paris. We were called upon to help plan all aspects of the wedding reception in Atlanta for family and friends, and our bride wanted her reception to reflect her Parisian experiences.

Plans began in earnest with the invitation. We utilized the concept of travel postcards as the foundation for the invitation. We had the bride handwrite her and her husband-to-be's travel itinerary, apprising all the invitees of just where they would be and when, so that the invitees could have a feeling of attachment to the actual ceremony.

Invitation done, we set out to design the food and beverage for the reception. We had one major obstacle. The couple were militant vegan vegetarians. However, the culinary department of A

Legendary Event created the perfect eight-course vegan buffet reception, complete with vegan wedding cake!

More Award-Winning Events

For more information on other award-winning events, and perhaps for some inspiration for your own, check out the following websites:

Canadian Event Industry Awards:
www.canadianspecialevents.com

Event Solutions Magazine's Spot Light Awards:
www.event-solutions.com

International Special Events Magazine's Gala Awards:
www.specialevents.com

International Special Events Society Esprit Awards:
www.ises.com

Meeting Professional Awards and Global Paragon Awards:
www.mpiweb.org

17
A Final Word: Growing and Enjoying Your Business

We hope this book has armed you with all the information you need to start a rewarding and prosperous business in the special events industry. It will take time for your business to grow, but this book should give you a solid start. Our goal in writing this book is to share the experience we have gained through years of working in the world of special events with those who are just starting out. By doing so, we hope to help promote excellence in the industry. We want to help new event planning businesses avoid some of the common mistakes and gain an advantage from knowing some hints and trade secrets. We want you to succeed.

It will be hard work, which we're sure you can see from reading through this guide. Your life will be busy if you want your business to prosper. Committing to your business will require some personal sacrifices along the way. Be clear about your goals and expectations, and make smart decisions that will allow you to grow as a person and as a business.

As your business grows, you will find that your days grow too, with endless phone calls to make and dozens of unread e-mails in your inbox. Remember that this is a business that relies on your creativity and energy. Take care of yourself. You may find, like many, that a good strategy is to schedule personal time into your calendar and keep those dates, for they are every bit as important as your business. You should book time to go to the gym or enjoy your favorite recreational activity. Get outdoors and meet friends for lunches and dinners. Your social life will remain an important part of being in business, so don't neglect the offers when they come in and don't make excuses to stay home and work. Most projects will allow you at least a couple of hours free a week!

As much as it may seem hard to do when you are just starting your own special events business, and even more so when you get busy, try to eat right and get enough sleep. You won't do yourself and your business any good if you wind up without the energy to carry out the work.

Make time to participate in industry associations. We know that association meetings seem to crop up when you are busy, and it is easy to find reasons not to attend. But these meetings are important to you and to the industry as a whole. This is where you can learn from the pros and offer your assistance to those who, like you, are just starting out.

The world of special events has changed dramatically since we first entered it — and it will continue to change with new trends, technological advances, and economic conditions. Continue to learn as your business grows. Take workshops and courses to develop your event planning skills and stay informed of new trends in the industry. Hone your other business skills through workshops on topics such as marketing, public speaking, and business writing.

Stay current on trends by subscribing to all the wonderful trade publications that are available to you. (See the appendix for a partial list.) Join your local board of trade or chamber of commerce, or at least attend a few networking or speaker functions. We also recommend that you attend industry conferences and trade shows each year, or at least every second year, where you will learn about the business and meet other industry professionals.

All of us should take pride in this industry and make it the best that it can be. We can do this only by sharing our experiences and by collectively working to improve the quality of the events we produce. We share a common pride in this industry, and we welcome you to join in. Congratulations on your decision to join what we consider to be the world's most enjoyable, vibrant, and fulfilling industry. And good luck. We look forward to meeting you.

APPENDIX:
Resources

Here is a list of event management professional associations, periodicals, conferences, award shows, business/government websites and software resources listed alphabetically. Please note that the information was current at the time of writing and is subject to change.

Professional Associations

Alliance of Meeting Management Companies (AMMC)
www.ammc.org

American Society of Association Executives (ASAE)
www.asaenet.org

Association of Certified Professional Wedding Consultants (ACPWC)
www.acpwc.com

Association of Collegiate Conference and Events Directors —
    International (ACCED)
acced-i.colostate.edu/imis_web/ScriptContent/Index.cfm

Association for Convention Marketing Executives (ACME)
www.acmenet.org

Association of Corporate Travel Executives (ACTE)
www.acte.org

Association of Destination Management Executives (ADME)
www.adme.org

Association for Events Management Education (AEME)
www.aeme.org

Association for Wedding Professionals International (AFWPI)
www.afwpi.com

Canadian Special Events Society (CSES)
www.cses.ca

Center for Exhibition Industry Research (CEIR)
www.ceir.org

Convention Industry Council (CIC)
www.conventionindustry.org

Hospitality Sales and Marketing Association International (HSMAI)
www.hsmai.org

Incentive Travel and Meetings Association (ITMA)
www.itma-online.org

Independent Meeting Planners Association of Canada (IMPAC)
www.impaccanada.com

International Association for Exhibition Management (IAEM)
www.iaem.org

International Associations of Fairs and Expositions (IAFE)
www.fairsandexpos.com

International Festival and Event Association (IFEA)
www.ifea.com

International Society of Meeting Planners (ISMP)
www.iami.org/ismp

International Special Events Society (ISES)
www.ises.com

Meeting Professionals International (MPI)
www.mpiweb.org

National Association of Catering Executives (NACE)
www.nace.net

National Speakers Association (NSA)
www.nsaspeaker.org

Professional Convention Management Association (PCMA)
www.pcma.org

Society of Government Meeting Professionals (SGMP)
www.sgmp.org

Society of Independent Show Organizers (SISO)
www.siso.org

Trade Show Exhibitors Association (TSEA)
www.tsea.org

Periodicals

Canadian Event Perspective Magazine
www.canadianspecialevents.com/CEP/home.html

Corporate Meetings & Incentives
cmi.meetingsnet.com

Event Solutions
www.event-solutions.com

EXPO
www.expoweb.com

Meetings & Conventions
www.meetings-conventions.com

Special Events Magazine
www.specialevents.com

Successful Meetings
www.successmtgs.com

Conventions/Conferences

UNITED STATES

Event Solutions Expo
Held annually — Summer
www.event-solutions.com/expo/expo2004/home.html

Eventworld — International Special Events Society
Held annually — Summer
www.ises.com

Expo! Expo! — International Association for Exhibition Management
Held annually — Winter
www.iaem.org

Professional Education Conference North America —
Professionals International
Held annually — January/February
www.mpiweb.org/education/pec

Special Event Conference and Trade Show
Held annually — Summer
www.thespecialeventshow.com

World Education Conference — Meeting Professionals International
Held annually — Summer
www.mpiweb.org/education

CANADA

Canadian Special Events and Meetings Expo
Held annually — Spring
Locations: Vancouver, Calgary, Toronto, Halifax
www.canadianspecialevents.com

Special Event Award Shows
UNITED STATES (international awards)

Esprit Awards Celebration — International Special Events Society
Held annually — Summer
www.ises.com

Special Events Magazine's Gala Awards
Held annually — Summer
www.specialevents.com/gala_awards

Spot Light Awards — Event Solutions
Held annually — Summer
www.event-solutions.com

CANADA

Canadian Event Industry Awards
Held annually — Spring
www.canadianspecialevents.com/ceia/ceia_home.html

Business and Government

Better Business Bureau
www.bbb.org

UNITED STATES

US Department of State
www.state.gov

The White House
www.whitehouse.gov

CANADA

Business Development Bank of Canada (BDC)
www.bdc.ca

Government of Canada
www.gc.ca

Software

Corbin Ball Associates
www.corbinball.com

Simply Accounting
www.simplyaccounting.com
or 1-800-773-5445 (United States and Canada)

Ultimate Technology Guide for Meeting Professionals
www.mpiweb.org/resources/mpif/purchase.asp

GLOSSARY

ACCOUNTS PAYABLE

Accounts owed by a business for supplies or services. Listed as a liability on the company's balance sheet.

ACCOUNTS RECEIVABLE

Accounts owing to a business for services provided and sold on credit. Listed as an asset on the company's balance sheet.

ACTION PLAN

A detailed schedule of the steps and time frames needed for carrying out a very specific element tied to an event.

BALANCE SHEET

A statement that provides a snapshot of a business's financial position at a set date, listing assets, liabilities, and net worth. Also called a statement of condition.

CONTINGENCY PLAN

A plan that thoroughly identifies potential issues and problems and methods for addressing each.

CRISIS MANAGEMENT

A process that identifies the potential crises that could take place during an event and defines methods for dealing with each.

CRITICAL PATH

A schedule that lists all the activities that are part of an event plan and assigns the minimum amount of time required for each. Also called a timeline or workback.

DEMOGRAPHICS

Statistics on population that relate socioeconomic factors such as age, family income, occupation, education, and so on.

ERGONOMICS

The field that studies the relationship between people and their working environment, especially with regard to safety and efficiency. Also called human engineering.

FIXED EXPENSES

Costs incurred by your business that remain constant regardless of how many events you produce or how many people attend a specific event.

GOAL

The overall desired result a client wishes to achieve.

MARKETING

Activities involved in the promotion for sale of goods or services, including market research and advertising.

MARKET RESEARCH

Research into the size, character, and potential of a given market for products or services to determine demands and opportunities.

NETWORKING

The exchange of information or services among individuals, groups, or institutions.

OBJECTIVE

A specific target that needs to be met in order to realize a client's goal.

OVERHEAD

All nonlabor expenses needed to operate a business.

REQUEST FOR PROPOSALS (RFP)

An invitation to companies and contractors to submit a proposal that will demonstrate the ability to deliver, in a cost-effective manner, on the objectives of a project.

TIME MANAGEMENT

Managing daily schedules and tasks to achieve maximum efficiency and productivity.

VARIABLE EXPENSES

Costs incurred by your business that vary depending on how many events you produce or how many people attend a specific event.